PRIMER contents

Francis Spufford's book *Unapologetic: Why, Despite Everything, Christianity Makes Surprising Emotional Sense* begins with a seven-page recital of everything wrong with Christians. It is a brilliant and bracing read:

UNAPOLOGETIC
WHY, DESPITE
EVERYTHING,
CHRISTIANITY
can still make
SURPRISING
EMOTIONAL
SENSE

"A RARE GEM, A BOOK THAT CARRIES CONVICTION BY BEING HONEST ALL THE WAY THROUGH."
JOHN GRAY, INDEPENDENT

FRANCIS SPUFFORD

Francis Spufford,
Unapologetic
(London: Faber
& Faber, 2013),
1-2, 5.

> We believe in a load of bronze-age absurdities... we're dogmatic, we're self-righteous... we fetishize pain and suffering... we're bleeding hearts who don't understand the wealth-creating powers of the market... we uphold the nuclear family, with all its micro-tyrannies and imprisoning stereotypes... we're the hairshirted enemies of the ordinary family pleasures of parenthood, shopping, sex, and car ownership... we think that everyone who disagrees with us is going to roast for all eternity... we cover up child abuse, because we care more about power than justice... we're the villains in history, on the wrong side of every struggle for human liberty.
>
> And worst... there is no reason for it... Most people's lives provide them with a full range of loves and hates and joys and despairs, and a moral framework by which to understand them, and a place for transcendence without any need for religion. Believers are people touting a solution without a problem, and an embarrassing solution too, a really damp-palmed, wide-smiling, can't-dance solution. In an anorak.

There is no point hiding from this, but we need not despair and we must not retreat. Instead, we need to think how best we can communicate the gospel in light of these caricatures, assumptions, and the genuine failings of the church to live up to its message.

The church has taken up this task from its very beginnings. We can read, for example, of Justyn Martyr, who wrote to the Roman Senate in the early second century to respond to the ill-treatment of Christians. He did so because *"when we are examined, we make no denial... we count it impious not to speak the truth in all things, which also we know is pleasing to God, and because we are also now very desirous to deliver you from an unjust prejudice."* That is, Justin feels compelled to speak God's truth for God's sake, and to do so as compellingly as possible, attempting to disarm "unjust prejudice." Formally or informally, whether addressing government authorities or our mates down the pub, this is the task of apologetics, and the topic of issue 07.

Justin Martyr, *Second Apology*, ch4.

Now that I've used the 'a' word for the first time, it is worth acknowledging that apologetics can prove to be theological marmite. Some people love the thought of engaging with culture and thinking how best to 'tear down strongholds' or 'subversively fulfil' the latest trends. Others, as Dan Strange notes in the first article, find apologetics far more intimidating or suspect that it distracts from actually getting on with evangelism and betrays a lack of confidence in God's sufficient word.

In light of this, let me highlight the shape of this issue of *Primer* and how we've reflected on and addressed those concerns. First, we start with Dan Strange, who argues that our engagement with the world needs to be shaped by what the Bible reveals about the world. The heart of his article is a discussion of what the Bible says fallen human beings are like. Quite intentionally then, we let the Bible set the agenda for our evangelistic questions and methods.

Next, we asked Matt Peckham to be your guide to several recent books on apologetics. It's an introductory tour of many of the best resources, including some very recent and significant works on the relationship between knowledge and faith. One of the great things here is the way that we're equipped to go and ask questions, rather than woodenly presenting our case or feeling that we're the only ones who need to come up with answers.

For our regular historical piece we have an excerpt from Blaise Pascal's *Pensées* – a published scrapbook of his thoughts on reason, miracles, happiness, and the centrality of Jesus to anything we have to say. Pascal hoped to work them into a defence of Christianity before his untimely death aged 39. In the form they have come down to us, they provide an intriguing and mysterious stream of thought and so William Edgar comes alongside to introduce them and reflect with us on their significance.

All three of these articles reject the idea that apologetics is some lofty and intellectualised pursuit, and the rest of *Primer* 07 is designed to reinforce that view. Jonathan Leeman's article is a vital piece of the puzzle because it draws the church into the conversation. Jesus spoke about the apologetic power of the church community – the way our love for one another makes the gospel visible – and yet this is regularly overlooked in discussions around apologetics. In the words of our title, the task is to *show and tell* the gospel.

And then we wanted to focus on how we can integrate apologetics into regular ministry life. Gavin McGrath discusses apologetics and preaching, arguing that Scripture seeks to persuade us and subvert our assumptions about the world. Seen that way, apologetics and exegesis (the careful study and explanation of a text) are not enemies but bedfellows, to the extent that I want to start talking about *apolegesis*. But that's probably just me.

Finally, to really bring the theme home, we have interviewed a number of churches about how they are engaging apologetically with their communities – what are the questions they face, how have they learnt to answer them, and how are they living out the gospel in compelling ways? It makes for a very encouraging read! We have included three interviews here in issue 07 and you can find more at *Primerhq.com*.

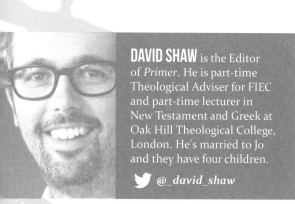

DAVID SHAW is the Editor of *Primer*. He is part-time Theological Adviser for FIEC and part-time lecturer in New Testament and Greek at Oak Hill Theological College, London. He's married to Jo and they have four children.

🐦 *@_david_shaw*

PROPERLY

UNDERSTOOD,

CHRISTIANITY IS

BY NO MEANS

THE OPIATE OF

THE PEOPLE.

IT'S MORE LIKE THE

SMELLING SALTS.

Tim Keller, The Prodigal God: Recovering
the Heart of the Christian Faith

5

An Unholy Mess

how our view of human nature shapes apologetics

For many, the discipline of 'apologetics' still remains something of a dark art.

DANIEL STRANGE is College Director and Tutor in Culture, Religion, and Public Theology at Oak Hill College. He is the author of *Their Rock is Not Like Our Rock: A Theology of Religions*, and writes a regular editorial for *Themelios*. Dan is an elder at East Finchley Baptist Church.

I often meet three kinds of people for whom that is true:

The Scared associate apologetics with brainy academic and often scientific types. They wouldn't know a 'cosmological argument' if it came up and bit them. As a result, while they want to defend their faith, they can feel inferior and ill-equipped.

Then there are *The Sceptics*. They worry that apologetics is 'worldly' in that it tries to escape the foolishness of the cross (1 Cor 1:18), relying on human reason and denying the agency and power of the Holy Spirit. Moreover, apologetics can be seen as a distraction from evangelism, from expounding the word and preaching Christ and him crucified.

Of course, sometimes you stumble upon *The Schooled*. They are well up on the apologetic methodology, the warring tribes associated with it, and the minutiae that are rehearsed on various blogs and message boards, but they probably haven't had a significant in-the-flesh apologetic conversation with a non-Christian for years.

Not only have I taught apologetic courses at Oak Hill for over a decade but I've been giving an apology for apologetics (or rather my take on it!) which seeks to satisfy the concerns of *Scared*, *Sceptic*, and *Schooled* alike. That's what I'll be seeking to do in this article, arguing that a biblical view of humanity encourages us to engage in apologetics, and that it informs our methods.

To begin with, as a working definition we'll run with Oliphint's:

> **Christian apologetics is the application of biblical truth to unbelief.**

K. Scott Oliphint, *Covenantal Apologetics: Principles & Practices in Defense of Our Faith* (Wheaton: Crossway, 2013), 29.

It might be helpful to mention various perspectives of the apologetic task: vindication, defence, refutation, and persuasion. Finally, we can speak of various apologetic 'families,' such as *Classical*, *Evidentialist*, *Fideistic*, and *Presuppositional*.

See next page for definitions...

CLASSICAL - Arguments based on logic, often to prove that God necessarily exists. In a nutshell: *Belief is reasonable.*

EVIDENTIALIST - Arguments based on evidence (for e.g. creation, the reliability of the Bible, the resurrection of Jesus). *The facts are on our side.*

FIDEISTIC - This approach is much more sceptical about the value of arguments since God confounds the wisdom of the world. Oftentimes, the result is to emphasise the need for faith to understand and the priority of proclaiming the gospel. *Unbelief is so unreasonable that only the gift of faith can overcome it.*

PRESUPPOSITIONALIST - Based on the view that classical and evidentialist approaches are too optimistic about human ability to embrace the truth, and that fideists are too pessimistic, presuppositionalists aim to confront unbelievers with the unworkability of their own basic assumptions about the world and to invite them to see the world from a Christian perspective. *There is no objective place to argue from, but what God has revealed can be used to appeal to unbelievers still made in his image.*

There is overlap, of course: many people integrate several approaches, and there is debate over where individual theologians fit.

For a really helpful in-depth discussion of these approaches see Kenneth D. Boa & Robert M. Bowman Jr, *Faith Has Its Reasons: An Integrative Approach to Defending Christianity* 2nd ed. (Paternoster, 2006). This text is available in full and for free online at *bible.org/series/faith-has-its-reasons*.

Coming straight to the point, I'm not going to argue for a new way, or to suggest you join a new family. I am of the firm belief that it is the *presuppositional* family of apologetics that best builds on the foundation of Reformed theology.

The presuppositional family traces its lineage from Calvin to Abraham Kuyper to Cornelius Van Til and then onto various diverse offspring (with their own disciples), **including** Greg Bahnsen, John Frame, Richard Pratt, Bill Edgar, Doug Wilson, Ted Turnau, and Tim Keller.

It's a matter of heated debate whether Francis Schaeffer can be classed as a presuppositionalist, and C.S. Lewis in equal degrees of delight and frustration seems to inhabit all the apologetic schools at various times including many presuppositional statements.

While I would admit that, at times, its PR could have been better (perceived as being unapplied and unappealingly intellectualist), I want to argue that presuppositionalism most satisfactorily answers John Frame's question, "What sort of defence will best glorify our God (cf. 1 Cor 10:31)?" and that presuppositionalism is truest to the biblical account of fallen 'image bearers.'

A Messy Mankind

Human beings are made up of a messy mixture. Paul admits as much when in Acts 17:22 he calls the Athenians 'very religious' (in Greek, *deisidaimonesterous*). This term appears only once in the New Testament and scholars and commentators interpret it differently: is it a positive acknowledgment of piety or a negative denunciation of ignorant superstition? Maybe, though, it's both:

Bahnsen, *Always Ready: Directions for Defending the Faith* (Texas: Covenant Media Foundation, 1996), 254.

> *It is not beyond possibility that Paul cleverly chose this term precisely for the sake of its ambiguity. His readers would wonder whether the good or bad sense was being stressed by Paul, and Paul would be striking a double blow: men cannot eradicate a religious impulse within themselves (as the Athenians also demonstrate), and yet this good impulse has been degraded by rebellion against the living and true God (as the Athenians also demonstrate). Although men do not acknowledge it, they are aware of their relation and accountability to the living and true God who created them. But rather than comes to terms with him and his wrath against their sin (cf. Rom 1:18), they pervert the truth. And in this they become ignorant and foolish (Rom 1:21-22).*

Deisidaimonesterous neatly captures the complexity of a biblical-theological anthropology. We might summarise it as follows. From Gen 3:15 onwards, God's sovereign judicial curse is to put enmity between the "seed of the woman" and the "seed of the Serpent:" two streams of humanity in complete opposition to one another. Reformed theologians call this the doctrine of the *antithesis* (lit. 'to set against'). This antithesis is captured in a wealth of stark biblical contrasts seen in genealogical patterns in the Old Testament (immediately in terms of Adam to Seth / Cain to Lamech), and described in the New Testament as the stark difference between death and life; darkness and light; blindness and sight; being in Adam and in Christ; goats and sheep; as covenant breakers and covenant keepers. Jesus declared that "no man can serve two masters" (Matt 6:24) and so "Whoever is not with me is against me" (Matt 12:30). Colossians 2:6-8 describes these two forms of existence when it speaks of those "rooted and built up in Christ" and those captive to "hollow and deceptive philosophy, which depends on human tradition and the elemental spiritual forces, *and not according to Christ*."

i.e. The Bible's account of human beings.

The antithesis is comprehensive and extends to all areas of human life: head, heart and hands. There is nothing that remains untouched or untainted. A religious antithesis generates an intellectual antithesis: "The *mind* governed by the flesh is hostile to God; it does not submit to God's law, nor can it do so." (Rom 8:7), and "once you were alienated from God and were enemies in your *minds* because of your evil behaviour" (Col 1:21).

Romans 1 reflects both the antithesis and this all-encompassing corruption. The fall signifies false worship as Paul says in Rom 1:23: we "exchanged the glory of the immortal God for images made to look like a mortal human being and birds and animals and reptiles." We are inescapably worshippers. There is a spiritual core to human beings, which means we either worship the living triune God, or we worship a counterfeit idol. There are no alternatives and there is no middle ground. It is worship of the Creator or worship of something created. Moreover, this worship is not simply an intellectual pursuit but includes the whole integrated person and their faculties – reason, emotion, will and imagination. False worship causes us to degenerate into futile thinking, darkened hearts (1:21) and corrupted desires (1:24, 29-31). This means, as David Naugle says, that *"at root, human beings are to be defined 'kardioptically,'"* that is, according to their hearts.

Worldview: The History of A Concept (Grand Rapids: Eerdmans, 2002), 291.

Given the truth of the antithesis, the implications for apologetics would seem to be stark. If the antithesis is true, then where is the point of contact between believer and unbeliever in their antithetical worlds? There can be no neutral ground, evidence, reasons, or facts which are not interpreted for Christ or against Christ. Is apologetics, therefore, a dead discipline because there is no continuity between believer and unbeliever? Well, thankfully no, because alongside the antithesis we have to add several other concepts.

Just as those rooted and built up in Christ still struggle with the sinful nature (producing fruit that looks like it belongs to a different tree), so analogously those "not according to Christ" are kept from fully expressing their rebellion and hatred of him. Van Til states this well:

> The natural [unregenerate] man, 'sins against' his own essentially Satanic principle. As the Christian has the incubus of his 'old man' weighing him down and therefore keeping him from realizing the 'life of Christ' within him, so the natural man has the incubus of the sense of Deity weighing him down and keeping him from realizing the life of Satan within him. The actual situation is therefore always a mix of truth with error. Being 'without God in the world' the natural man yet knows God, and, in spite of himself, to some extent recognizes God. By virtue of their creation in God's image, by virtue of the ineradicable sense of deity within them and by virtue of God's restraining general grace, those who hate God yet, in a restricted sense, know God, and do good.

Cornelius Van Til, *An Introduction to Systematic Theology* (Phillipsburg: P&R, 2007), 27.

It is the persistence of the *imago Dei* (the image of God), and, in Calvin's phrase, the *sensus divinitatis* (the sense of the divine) together with God's **common grace** which must be held in tension with the doctrine of the antithesis. There is no neat way of articulating this anthropological messiness, although as I've said *deisidaimonesterous* might capture it. Some of Van Til's more concise statements are helpful in us trying to understand:

That is, the kindness that God shows to his whole creation, sustaining it and restraining evil.

> *The natural man does not know God. But to be thus without knowledge, without living, loving, true knowledge of God, he must be one who knows God in the sense of having the sense of deity (Romans 1).*
>
> *The natural man is such a one as constantly throws water on a fire he cannot quench,*
>
> *The Prodigal cannot altogether stifle his Master's voice.*

Bahnsen, *Van Til's Apologetic: Readings and Analysis* (Phillipsburg: P&R, 1998), 447, 438, 459.

However, even Van Til admits to the struggle:

> *We cannot give any wholly satisfactory account of the situation... All that we can do with this question as with many other questions in theology, is to hem it in, in order to keep out errors, and to say that the truth lies within a certain territory.*

Van Til, *An Introduction to Systematic Theology*, 26.

A Method to Match the Mess

So what is presuppositionalism, and how is the presuppositional method able to most accurately describe and reflect the theological anthropology outlined above? Presuppositions are foundational truths that are self-evident and self-authenticating. You can't dig beneath them or take them to a higher authority.

> *At times we accept something, not because we can directly prove it, but because of the impossibility of the contrary. We cannot prove a certain position, but we can show that the inevitable consequences of rejecting that position are simply unthinkable.*

Grover Gunn, *Lectures on Apologetics* (Greenville: Southern Presbyterian Press, 1997).

It is from these presuppositions or ultimate commitments that this apologetic family takes its name because this is where our apologetic efforts need to be focused. It's not that presuppositionalism is *against* the use of evidentialist arguments. Indeed the Reformed doctrine of revelation recognises that *everything* that God has created is evidence for the God who is. However, it strongly critiques a naïve use of evidence that does not recognise the determining interpreting power of our ultimate commitments which are either to Christ, or something else. In one of his more feisty statements Van Til notes the following:

Cornelius Van
Til, *The Defence
of the Faith*,
122.

Apologetics, like systematics, is valuable to the precise extent that it presses the truth upon the attention of the natural man. The natural man must be blasted out of his hideouts, his caves, his lurking places. Neither Roman Catholic nor Arminian methodologies [associated with the Traditional Method of apologetics] have the flame-throwers with which to reach him. In the all-out war between the Christian and the natural man as he appears in modern garb it is only the atomic energy of a truly Reformed methodology that will explode the last Festung *[fortress] to which the Roman Catholic and the Arminian always permit him to retreat and to dwell in safety.*

In presuppositionalism this flame-thrower is called the *transcendental argument*, or the *transcendental thrust*. A transcendental argument does not try to set our worldviews aside and occupy some neutral ground, but rather to set them side-by-side and see which best fits the world. Grover Gunn likens our worldviews to a set of weighing scales in which we weigh the matters of life and what we believe to be true and good and worthy of our worship. As we have noted, the Bible does not think that unbelievers need some more evidence putting onto their scales to tip them towards belief. Instead the scales which they trust implicitly are faulty and need replacing. To convince people of that, we need an indirect argument. You can't expose faulty scales by weighing them. Instead, you put some officially verified weights on your scales. If your scales show that the 5kg weight weighs more than the 10kg weight then something has gone wrong with the scales. So then,

Grover Gunn,
*Lectures on
Apologetics*.

What we do in apologetics is to challenge people to weigh the basic issues of life on the scale of their world view. We challenge them to be honest in acknowledging the logical and consistent implications of their view of reality. We challenge them to compare these readings with what they know to be true in their heart of hearts, even if they will not consciously admit it... The non-Christian at times wants to believe that his world view scales register the weight which that testimony deep in his heart says it should register. Presuppositionalists call this "operating on borrowed capital." The atheist rejects God, but he wants to believe that he nevertheless has a consistent basis for morality and aesthetics and logic and science. The presuppositionalist pressures the non-Christian to read his scales honestly.

In his presuppositional primer, *Every Thought Captive*, Richard Pratt helpfully speaks of the 'two-step' strategy of presuppositionalism based on Prov 26:4-5:

Prov 26:4-5

Answer not a fool according to his folly,
lest you be like him yourself.
Answer a fool according to his folly,
lest he be wise in his own eyes.

Verse 4 encapsulates the "argument from truth." Like one standing on the rock of God's word, (cf. Matt 7:24-25) the Christian must not reason with the assumptions of the non-Christian or else they will become like the fool who does right in their own eyes. Apologetically this won't help anyone. Rather the Christian is one who in their hearts reveres Christ as Lord (1 Pet 3:15). We argue *for* Christianity *from* Christianity.

Pratt, *Every Thought Captive,* 86.

Verse 5 encapsulates the "argument from folly." For the sake of argument we must rehearse what it's like to stand on the sinking sand of our own autonomous commitment, judgments and the authorities we put in place of the living God (cf. Matt 7:26-27). We want fools to see the error of being wise in their own eyes. We must show them the outcome of what happens when their commitments are fully realised. In all of this we are appealing to what unbelievers know but have suppressed in their rebellion.

ibid., 92.

Ted Turnau recounts a good example of this:

I am indebted to Ted Turnau for this example, from our personal correspondence.

Back in the days of Apartheid, I had a friend who was studying photography. He told me over dinner that he wanted to go to South Africa.

"What for? It's incredibly dangerous there!"

"Because someone has to show the world what's going on there!"

"And what's going on there?"

"Black people are being treated like dogs!"

"And what's wrong with that?"

"WHAT?"

"I mean, I agree with you that it's wrong. I'm just interested in why *you* think it's wrong."

"What do you mean?"

"Well, why is it wrong to treat a black person like a dog? How are human beings different than dogs, that you should care more about them?"

And he couldn't give me an answer. His worldview, though strongly felt, had no answer about what made a human being different. And then I was able to share with him what the Christian worldview said about humans being made in God's image, and so they are to be treated with the utmost respect and care, more so than dogs. Doing a transcendental critique is playing the 3-year-old, asking why at places where most of us simply assume. Asking for transcendental justification means asking people to be willing to think outside the box and question assumptions in ways they may feel is inappropriate. But much of that inappropriateness comes from the failure to think things through thoroughly. It must be done with care, because done wrongly, it can be brutal and can lead to nothing more than resentment. Done gently, it can open up spaces that non-believers have never considered, and start rocking their own perspective.

A similar approach was commended by the German Lutheran theologian Helmut Thielicke. Ministering during and after the Second World War, he argued strenuously against what he saw as a defensiveness in 'traditional' apologetics that attempted to answer the questions of unbelievers. Instead, Thielicke notes that in the Garden of Eden, and throughout Scripture, particularly in the pastoral conversations of Christ, it is *God* who initiates and asks questions in a subversive yet persuasive way. For him, apologetics is an offensive exercise that "turns the tables" and thus challenges sinful men and women. He writes:

Helmut Thielicke, *Between God and Satan* (Grand Rapids: Eerdmans, 1961), 26. Quoted in Jeffrey Hamm, *Turning the Tables on Apologetics: Helmut Thielicke's Reformation of Christian Conversation* (Oregon: Pickwick, 2018), 130. Hamm's is a thoughtful and illuminating study of Thielicke's method which brings to the surface many of the issues discussed in this article.

Quoted in Hamm, 144.

So we see how wrong the view of 'apologetics' is, if it always understands itself only as the Answerer and not the Questioner. The Church of Jesus Christ, in the name of God, has much more to ask the world than it has to answer. The Christian faith is by no means a simple or straightforward answer to the life problems of religious people. Jesus does not respond, so to speak, rather he first of all poses the deepest questions. And this mode of the counterquestion approach should also preserve our message.

Christ's conversation with the Rich Young Ruler (Mark 10:17-22) is perhaps the supreme example of this method and merits careful reflection.

Back to Those Sceptics

In defending presuppositionalism I am sensitive to the charge that it's seen to be all too complicated and rationalistic.

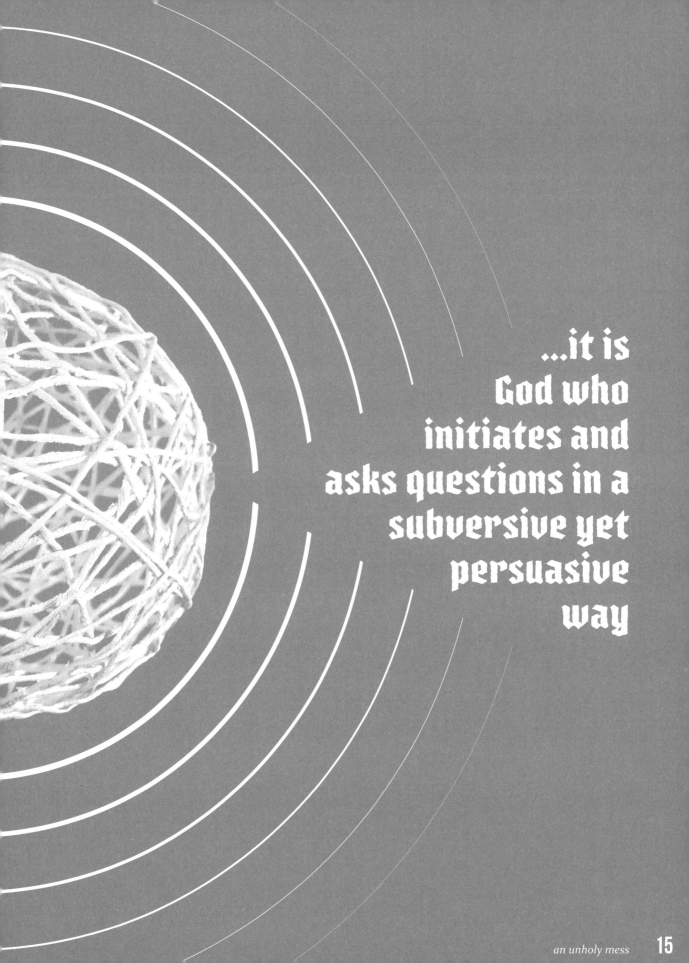

...it is
God who
initiates and
asks questions in a
subversive yet
persuasive
way

The Australian NT scholar Peter Bolt wrote a blog post a few years back which I'm pretty certain had in his crosshairs a talk I myself had given at that year's *Evangelical Ministry Assembly*:

> " *Once upon a time in a land far away, I heard a speaker at a conference insisting that evangelism ought to engage with the cultures around us. The task seemed so complicated. Mapping conceptual worlds. Integrating lofty ideas into unseen mental frameworks. And all of this was to be done well before you open your mouth about Jesus. Everyone I spoke with at morning tea had been thoroughly convinced of one thing: they could never do the kind of thing the speaker was calling for. And most of them were ministers who had gone through a full theological education! What hope would the unlettered and ordinary amongst us have (as the apostles were called, Acts 4:13)?*

Peter Bolt, 'Evangelism: The Simplicity of Changing the World', see www.moore.edu.au/resource/evangelism-the-simplicity-of-changing-the-world

In response I would want to say that apologetics is only as simple or complicated as the anthropology that underlies it. In Acts the apostles are seen to refute, argue and prove (see 9:22, for example). Paul at the Areopagus demonstrates this *par excellence* in that he appeals to the suppressed truth of the pagan poets, clearly setting side-by-side the transcendently unique Creator Yahweh and the nature of his creation, in contrast to the worldview of the Athenians. Acts seems to be full of transcendental thrust and two-step strategy, not as a substitute for preaching Christ but as a support.

Keller's 2018 address at the *National Parliamentary Prayer Breakfast* is to my mind a great example of cultural presuppositional apologetics. See *nationalprayerbreakfast.org.uk*

However, I would admit that the presuppositional family have not always helped themselves because they have failed to reflect a biblical anthropology which treats people as more than just brains on sticks. This does need addressing and recently has been in the writing and ministry of those such as Ted Turnau and Tim Keller.

The point was made nearly twenty-five years ago, though, by one of my apologetic heroes, Bill Edgar. He writes,

> " *Presuppositional apologetics, I believe, recognises the religious core of our natures better than other systems do, because it understands that we are united, and that our dispositional complex, however individual and diverse, is always directed towards a goal, be it the true hope of the gospel or the deceptive promise of the idol.*

Edgar, 'Without Apology: Why I Am a Presuppositionalist,' 20. I recently saw this seminal piece turning up as set reading for a *Biblical Counselling UK* module which reflects its holistic emphasis.

Given what we've said above about humans as worshippers, there's a sense in which presuppositions are only part of the picture. We have presuppositions (beliefs) but also predispositions (patterns of life) and predilections (feelings). This is important because it means that the conflict generated by the antithesis and the enduring image of God isn't only worked out on the intellectual level. The *sensus divinitatis* (Rom 1:18-20) is the suppressed awareness of a *broken relationship*. The tension people feel between their worldview commitments and the way they actually live their lives isn't just an intellectual tension. People live their lives seeking hope and love and comfort and dignity, even though their worldview cannot ground those desires and their idols cannot satisfy them. Put like this, it's not hard to fold the keen insights of scholars like Charles Taylor and his work on our secular age into an explicitly presuppositional framework. All of a sudden, *deisidaimonesterous* is wonderfully insightful as we walk around and look carefully at our culture's objects and discern our 'unknown gods.' And we see them *everywhere*. The secular is indeed haunted, as encapsulated by the opening sentence of Julian Barnes' book, *Nothing to Be Frightened Of*, "I don't believe in God, but I miss Him."

In noting this we are, inexorably, pulled back by the magnet that is 1 Peter 3:15, arguably the *classic text* for presuppositionalism:

1 Pet 3:15 | *But in your hearts revere Christ as Lord. Always be prepared to give an answer to everyone who asks you to give the reason for the hope that you have.*

Giving an answer (*apologia*) readily takes on the sense of a reasoned defence, as in a court of law. But what are we giving a reason for? That there is a god? That Jesus existed? That the Bible is true? That Christianity is the only true religion? No, we are giving a reason for "hope"– the hope in us. The hope in the gospel of Christ.

And how do we communicate hope? In lots and lots of ways not only in intellectual argument. Think of a girl confronted by a boy who wants to ask her out. She might say "give me a good reason why I should go out with you." Now imagine her reaction if the boy's answer is purely intellectual, "If you quantify the fun to time ratio of spending time with me, I think you'll agree that it compares favourably with similar ratios of spending any time with any boy at school. Here, allow me to adduce historical evidence to support my claim." There are better answers that could be given "I love you; let me paint a picture of where life might take us…"

We are not brains on sticks but whole people who feel, will, imagine – and the reason for our hope can operate on all those levels. If you're not an 'intellectual' you are not disqualified for giving a reason for hope. We have hope, and many people today are hope-less. We are whole people talking to other whole people and introducing them not merely to a "philosophy" or a "worldview" or even a "message" (although the gospel is all three), but a *person*. The old King James translation of Acts 8:35 gets this sense well: "Then Philip opened his mouth, and began at the same scripture, and preached unto him Jesus."

The combination of confrontation and appeal I have been recommending is not just limited to a few proof-texts. As a number of New Testament scholars have argued, it is built into the whole of Luke and Acts, given the way that those books draw on **the idolatry passages in Isa 40-55**. In those chapters the Holy One of Israel is contrasted to the worthless idols built and worshipped by the surrounding nations. In chapter 44 Isaiah ridicules the idolater who out of one block of wood makes both his god and the fire for his evening meal:

See e.g., David W. Pao, *Acts and the Isaianic New Exodus* (Grand Rapids: Baker Academic, 2000); Kenneth D Litwak, *Echoes of Scripture in Luke-Acts: Telling the History of God's People Intertextually* (Edinburgh: T&T Clark, 2005). There is also Flavien Pardigon's unpublished dissertation: *Paul Against the Idols: The Areopagus Speech and Religious Inclusivism* (PhD diss. Westminster Theological Seminary, 2008).

Isa 44:18-19

They know nothing, they understand nothing;
their eyes are plastered over so that they cannot see,
and their minds closed so that they cannot understand.
No one stops to think,
no one has the knowledge or understanding to say,
'Half of it I used for fuel;
I even baked bread over its coals,
I roasted meat and I ate.
Shall I make a detestable thing from what is left?
Shall I bow down to a block of wood?'

This confrontation, however, is in the context of the Lord's appeal to his people to experience forgiveness and restoration in a new exodus. Those are the promises that animate Luke-Acts, and those two themes (confrontation and invitation) climax in many ways in Acts 17 with Paul's revulsion at idolatry and call for repentance.

Paul, then, becomes a model for our engagement. In our day, no one stops to think. Most people we know don't think about apologetics or culture, or worship, or ways of viewing the world, or idolatry. They are just living their lives. They don't stop to think. The aim of presuppositional apologetics is to get them to stop and think – to try and rouse them from a living nightmare and bring them back to reality, back to their senses. The idols we worship can't and don't deliver what they promise on any level; either intellectually, emotionally or imaginatively. They can't give satisfying ultimate explanations of the world. Our task is to make people stop and think about their self-deception. To make them stop and think about the commitments they make, the authorities they listen to, the stories and scripts they follow. And from here it's only a short step to get to Jesus.

Joel Garver, 'A Primer on Presuppositionalism,' from the author's website, but currently unavailable online

....once a person has been made aware of the inadequacies of her false covenant lords, the true Covenant Lord, who is always faithful, even through suffering (as demonstrated on the cross), can be commended. At this point evidence (much of which has been there all along) may take on a new cast or be open to new ways of seeing. It may be possible for the person to see what a new set of commitments might mean and how, given those commitments, the existence of God and trust in him could be rational, evidentially plausible, and satisfying. The goal of apologetics, then, is not to win an argument, but to commend the Saviour as the one in whom human life, personal relationships, and knowledge can find rest. The epistemological and related issues are only part of a much bigger picture.

Questions for further thought and discussion

1. What does Dan think Paul might mean when he tells the Athenians that they are "very religious"?

2. Where in Scripture do we see evidence of the 'antithesis'? And where in Scripture can you find evidence of the image of God enduring in fallen men and women?

3. How do these ideas create a helpful account of human beings?

4. How do these ideas shape our expectations and methods in evangelism?

5. Why is it important to think about people as worshippers and hopers rather than simply as thinkers?

In Defence of Madmen

Apologetics through the lens of four recent books

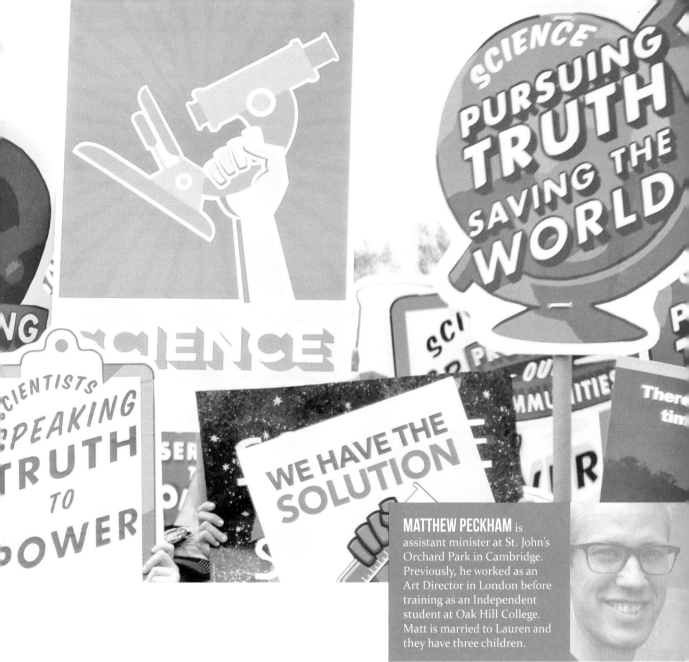

MATTHEW PECKHAM is assistant minister at St. John's Orchard Park in Cambridge. Previously, he worked as an Art Director in London before training as an Independent student at Oak Hill College. Matt is married to Lauren and they have three children.

A couple of years back, an interview with the TV personality and actor James Corden pressed him on his spiritual beliefs. When asked to define his own faith, Corden replied:

I don't know what it is, other than a hunch. Ultimately, if you were to say 'what are my beliefs?' I'd really struggle, because... you can't argue with science and I don't – only a madman would.

John Bishop In Conversation With... (UKTV, 2016).

Corden's response reveals two striking things that reflect today's society. Firstly, it clearly articulates the modern mindset that sees an insurmountable divide between 'belief' and 'facts.' Secondly, Corden's visible unease in answering highlights the social taboo of attempting to reconcile the two in a world where science claims the monopoly on true knowledge – the 'facts.'

A consequence of Enlightenment thinking, this view positions belief as an unverifiable value and therefore a matter of doubt, not fact – a point explored in Lesslie Newbigin's *The Gospel in a Pluralist Society*. In addition, as Newbigin noted, the acceptability of facts over values is such that values are consequently confined to the private sphere. In the public eye, "we don't do God." In private we may believe different things, but in public we are united around the facts – a situation only compounded by a post-9/11 caution toward public religious debate on the one hand, and the aggressive rise of so-called **new Atheism** on the other. This poses a real challenge to the pursuit of both apologetics and the proclamation of the gospel – how do we go about making a compelling case for the Christian faith in the public sphere, the realm of 'facts'?

Lesslie Newbigin, *The Gospel In A Pluralist Society* (London: SPCK, 1989). Central to the Enlightenment was an emphasis on human reason and scepticism about anything that could not be scientifically observed or logically proved.

Alastair Campbell's famous comment about the Tony Blair government. It should be noted – as some point out, and others find out to their cost – that our current cultural climate blurs the boundary of public and private (with social media platforms and the like). However, whilst this is true in terms of environment, it remains the case that there is still a divide conceptually between that which has collective acceptance, and that which remains mere personal preference, regardless of where and how it is expressed.

Not so new anymore, the phrase first appeared in 2007 to describe a movement spearheaded by Richard Dawkins, Christopher Hitchens, Sam Harris and Daniel Dennett.

Newbigin, *The Gospel In A Pluralist Society*, 10.

On one level, the answer seems obvious: we proclaim the gospel as fact, because it is, and we deploy apologetics to support the reasonableness of this claim in the face of objection. However, I think Newbigin would warn us here against accepting the rationalist premise: **submitting revelation to the bar of reason**. Where an enlightened attitude crowns individual human reason and rationality as the arbiter of truth, a Christian response may well be to accept the challenge: "Reason and rationality you say? We've got that in spades! Let me prove it to you…" But we need to be cautious.

Traditional apologetics, be it the classical approach (an appeal to logical proofs) or the evidentialist approach (an appeal to empirical evidence), usually operate in the realm of logic and facts as though it were neutral territory. This is the assumption of the unbeliever. Thus the believer accepts the invite of their unbelieving friend, seeking to occupy this neutral ground to thrash out what is true in the world. Both parties agree to suspend their beliefs simply to see where facts and reason lead to under these agreed conditions. Except of course that there is no neutral ground. The believer confesses Jesus as Lord, and the unbeliever cannot adopt a neutral posture: they are truth suppressors, and their total depravity includes their intellect, reason and logical operation. Yet, in pursuing this approach, the believer implicitly affirms the supremacy of "facts," risking further relegation of belief to the private sphere and the realm of doubt. This is a problem for gospel proclamation which – as Newbigin puts it – is an authoritative proclamation that invites *belief*. It is in light of this that many apologists adopt a presuppositional approach.

Newbigin, *The Gospel In A Pluralist Society*, 5-6.

This approach is grounded in Reformed convictions about the nature of human knowing: Although able to know God, humanity "suppresses the truth by their wickedness, since what may be made known about God is plain to them, because God has made it plain to them" (Rom 1:18-19). Sin, not ignorance, is the root of error, as Jesus tells the Pharisees, it is "*because* I tell you the truth you do not believe me" (John 8:45).

Being made in God's image, we know him, yet in our sin deny him. This is a radical self-deception. Such deception leads us to presuppose that we can discern truth and meaning apart from God, denying that the world already has a divinely revealed meaning (more on this later). As Cornelius Van Til puts it, *"the unbeliever assumes that interpreting the world is an original procedure, rather than a derivative one."* That is, we cut God out of the picture and like to imagine that we are imposing order and meaning on the world.

Cornelius Van Til, *Christian Apologetics*, ed. William Edgar, (Phillipsberg, NJ: P&R Publishing), 80.

This doesn't mean, however, that the unbeliever can't say anything true, or discover things about God's world. The point is that because it's God's world, it is only the biblical worldview within which the unbeliever is able to operate consistently.

The apologist then, seeks to expose this situation, gently pointing out the sheer unworkable premise of consistently denying God: bereft of Christian presuppositions, the unbeliever is a fork in a world of soup. In addition, by presupposing God and *beginning* with his revelation as authoritative, Christianity must then *"present itself as the light that makes the facts of human experience, and above all the nature of man himself, to appear for what they really are."*

Cornelius Van Til, *Christian Apologetics*, 86.

Whilst presuppositional apologetics can, and should, employ traditional arguments, the real opportunities – and issues – are seen when we understand ultimate commitments as foundational to worldview, and culture as a manifestation of worldview. It's well worth reflecting, then, on the role of culture and the critique of worldview explored by a presuppositional understanding.

For the rest of this article, I want to look at four books which will help expand these themes in a particular direction. Firstly, looking at the place of culture and practical engagement, and then moving on to a broader understanding of knowing, as it relates to belief. As we do so, we'll draw out two corresponding points which I hope will significantly inform our apologetic efforts: 1) Belief is shared and public, 2) facts rest on belief.

1. Engaging Culture & Worldview

What is cultural engagement?

William Edgar, *Created & Creating* (Downers Grove, IL: IVP Academic, 2017), 87.

Bill Edgar contends that *"cultural engagement before the living God is, along with worship, the fundamental calling of the human race."* This isn't, however, an argument for binge-watching reality TV box sets, as we shall (thankfully) see.

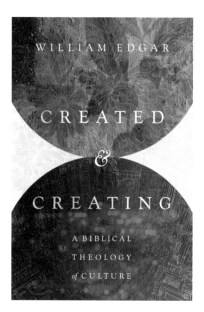

Created & Creating is written primarily for Christians, promoting the necessity of thinking these issues through. In doing so, Edgar gives a measured and biblical foundation for the legitimacy of cultural engagement. Whilst it's not an apologetic work *per se* (Edgar's written plenty of those), it presents the case for a view of culture as the outworking of the biblical mandate for image-bearing activity in God's world (Gen 1:27-30). What Edgar has in mind as 'cultural engagement' is not mere analysis, but the entirety of human activity – family, work, citizenship, agriculture, and artistic pursuits.

Edgar dedicates a sizeable slab of the book to Christian objections: Doesn't the Bible condemn the world and worldliness? Shouldn't we be resisting it? It's all going to burn anyway, right? Edgar answers these objections through the Creation-Fall-Redemption schema. The reason for doing this is twofold: firstly it underlines the distinction between creation and fall which he believes is missing from the "don't conform to the world" objection to cultural engagement. Edgar reminds us that what is morally corrupt is the direction our use of creation takes. In light of this, Edgar proposes that *"our duty to oppose cultural evil is not a war against creation but against the malignancy of sin."*

William Edgar, *Created & Creating*, 100.

Secondly, redemption reiterates the value of creation and brings about the undoing of sin within it. The redeemed are those for whom the cultural mandate has been republished. Drawing on the Great Commission, and detecting it in all four gospels, not just Matt 28:20, he links it to obedient discipleship through passages such as 1 Cor 10:31 (doing all to the glory of God). This leads Edgar to claim that for the redeemed, culture is *"the life of the new covenant, with its fruit bearing and proper dominion."*

William Edgar, *Created & Creating*, 219. It seems to me that returning to Genesis and the cultural mandate has to be the place to start, presenting the purpose of God in making humanity in his image. However, regarding the "republication" of the cultural mandate, Edgar's discussion would perhaps benefit from reflecting on the distinction between cultivating and multiplying. That might be a way of protecting the distinctively evangelistic call to multiply by making disciples.

There are many significant observations here. Perhaps most pertinently, as Edgar mentions at the outset, cultural studies *"arose within the vacuum created by the loss of a sense of the presence of God in the West."* We began to interpret culture without reference to religion. Bridging that divide is what drives Edgar's emphasis on culture's religious nature: culture is cultic. The apologetic value of this insight is dealt with in *Popologetics*.

William Edgar, *Created & Creating*, 23.

Setting the story straight

" *You needed meaning, so you reached for a story to make sense of it all and told it to yourself until you believed it, just like the humans do. Just like they always do.*

Max, in *Humans*, Season 3, Episode 7 (Kudos Film & Television, Channel 4, 2018).

The writers of Channel 4's drama about artificial intelligence, *Humans*, have identified a key trait of the human condition here – connecting meaning, story and self-deception. These themes also lie behind **Ted Turnau**'s theological and practical guide to analysing culture.

Popologetics defines pop culture broadly as all types of cultural works and activity that are shared and widely received. But the key factor here is the role such cultural works play. Turnau's argument is that *"popular-cultural works form 'worlds of meaning' for us to inhabit."* Simply put, we use cultural works, with their embedded worldview, to make sense of life – to construct and give value to our view of the world. Whether movies,

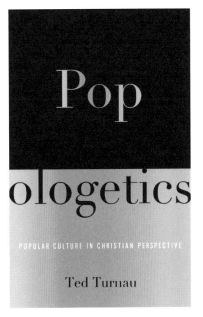

POPULAR CULTURE IN CHRISTIAN PERSPECTIVE

Ted Turnau

Ted Turnau, *Popologetics* (Phillipsburg, NJ: P&R Publishing, 2012), 19.

This doesn't require a popular work to include a narrative, such as a movie – rather every work contributes towards and is understood within narrative. This could be the modernist narrative of ignorance to enlightenment, or rags to riches story or the self-improvement story of humanism and so on.

As the narrator in Fight Club cynically puts it. *Fight Club* (20th Century Fox, 1999).

Turnau, *Popologetics*, 19.

Turnau is drawing on principles seen in Romans 1 and Psalm 19 here. Ted Turnau, *Popologetics*, 47 (emphasis original).

Turnau, *Popologetics*, 209.

products, trends or services, cultural works help narrate our understanding of the world – Who am I? Where am I going? What is my place in the world? (*"What kind of dining set defines me as a person...?"*) All such cultural works contribute in some way to these answers, providing *"shared worlds of meaning"* that narrate our own existence. In short, humans see reality as meaningful through stories.

Turnau demonstrates how such world-stories flow from presuppositions. These assumptions about the world, God and ourselves, inform and shape cultural works which in turn shapes our view of the world. This culture-making affirms and projects meanings of the world which are a distortion of the meaning God has already given it.

That creation finds it's meaning in God leads to an important understanding in the book: cultural activity is not simply creating meaning to fill a meaningless vacuum, rather we're *"responding to meaning that is already there, woven into creation."* In subduing creation we must rely on God's truths even to tell an alternative story. As Turnau reminds us: "meaningful human experience itself presupposes God." Although a distortion, in God's common grace, his goodness and truth are still evident, so that culture is *"the site of a messy mixture of grace and idolatry."*

So what is a *Popologetic*? Turnau's proposal (also termed a 'worldview apologetic'), uses simple diagnostic questions to discern the idolatry and truth within any given cultural phenomena. By analysing the stories and imaginative worlds projected by popular culture, Turnau shows how we can present the gospel as both a challenge and true, meaningful fulfilment of culture's pseudo-worship.

Think for a moment about Buzz and Woody from *Toy Story*. (Stick with me...) Buzz Lightyear is convinced of his own narrative that he is in fact a Space Ranger with fully workable, flying jet suit, commissioned to save the world. He believes it, he lives it out, he ignores or explains away any evidence to the contrary. It takes Woody to point out his faulty worldview, and explain to him the real narrative – *"You. Are. A. Toy!"* More than that, it is the 'true story' that ultimately fulfils Buzz's desire to be loved: He is loved precisely because he's a toy, who belongs to Andy.

Back in the real world, a *Popologetic* likewise engages the distorted stories people live by in order to set them straight. In doing so we can say of the gospel that it is *"the answer to the lies presented by the idols found in popular culture. It is the fulfilment of all the desires that motivate popular culture. It is the source of the good and true things that shine in popular culture."* In short, the shared beliefs evidenced around us can only be truly understood in relation to God and the gospel of Christ. Turnau's contention is that this should prompt us to see the breadth of the gospel that speaks to all of life (rather than restricted to abstract categories such as "salvation" or "ideas about God").

Turnau, *Popologetics*, 245.

Channeling your inner three year old

Worldviews may be formed and publicly expressed through cultural works, but they also exist at a more base level of beliefs and presuppositions. Such interpretations of the world are expressed in creeds the world unquestioningly lives by. "Evolution disproves God," "The Bible can say whatever you want," "You don't need God to have moral absolutes" are all such mantras. The reality is that such thinking doesn't hold up to scrutiny, yet is rarely challenged in daily conversation.

Tactics is really an extended handbook on exposing such wonky thinking. From different perspectives, **Greg Koukl** demonstrates how popular assumptions and plausibility structures quickly collapse under interrogation. In essence, this book attempts to demonstrate the value of a presuppositional approach in ways that feel refreshingly ordinary and accessible. Koukl's explicit intent is to equip the reader for diplomacy, to "manoeuvre effectively" in conversations of faith in the face of objections. His aim is not to convert but to disrupt the unbeliever's confidence in their assumptions, to *"put a stone in their shoe."* This is a kind of 'playing the three-year-old' approach; constantly asking the "why?" question. Why do you believe that? Why does that follow? etc.

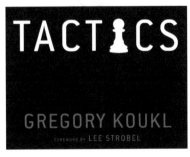

Gregory Koukl, *Tactics: A Game Plan For Discussing Your Christian Convictions* (Grand Rapids, MI: Zondervan, 2009), 38.

Koukl outlines his strategy, highlighting the need for questions for gathering information and leading the conversation. As he does, he also illuminates some helpful debating principles, such as distinguishing between forcefully stating a view, and reasoned argumentation. The second half of the book interacts with various types of objection (spotting self-defeating ideas, claims in contention with one another and so on). In all these interactions, Koukl believes we should have confidence in the necessity of biblical presuppositions to arrive at the truth: *"Christians have a powerful ally in the war of ideas: reality."*

Koukl, *Tactics*, 144. (Koukl is paraphrasing Francis Schaeffer here, from his book *The God Who Is There*).

Aside from being rhetorically useful, Koukl's strategy encourages conversations that consider more carefully what we think we know. This is really the heart of our apologetic leverage – how do we know what we know? However, addressing this question is all too often neglected by both non-Christians *and Christians* alike, and is worth reconsidering in more depth.

Esther Lightcap Meek, *Longing to Know* (Grand Rapids: Brazos Press, 2003).

Epistemology is the study of knowledge, asking how we know what we know.

MICHAEL POLANYI (1891-1976) was a Hungarian-British Scientist, whose major contribution was in questioning the scientific method. Polanyi proposes that we are situated beings, subjectively participating in the world, and that this is a fundamental factor in how we are able to acquire knowledge of it. We must move toward knowledge, through acts of dependence and trust, whether in a hypothesis, speculation, or the knowledge of others. His ideas can be summarised in his claim that all knowing is personal.

Objecting to objectivity

Intended for those considering Christianity, **Esther Meek**'s book *Longing to Know* tackles the question "can we know God?" by reconsidering the nature of knowing itself. At root, the failure of modern epistemology – as Meek points out – is its insistence on true knowledge as objective information 'out there' that we must acquire.

Drawing on the work of **Michael Polanyi**, Meek's claim is that when we examine what really happens in knowing something, it is demonstrably untrue that it is a purely objective process in which our subjective involvement and beliefs play no part. Such an understanding for example, doesn't adequately account for how we move from not knowing to knowing.

An alternative way forward recognises the act of knowing as a process.

This begins with *subsidiary* (or *tacit*) knowledge; peripheral clues that fall into three categories: evidence in the world, embodied knowing, and who we listen to. Such clues may include tangible evidence, testimony, worldview, or even a "hunch."

In our longing to know, we integrate these elements in an attempt to move toward *focal* knowledge – a personal conviction that we might describe as objective. Rather than academic, Meek intends this description of knowing to be very ordinary (think for example of how we come to know about balance – through theory, observation and personal embodiment). In short, *"knowing is the human act of making sense of experience."*

Meek, *Longing To Know*, 117.

Meek, however, isn't saying that truth is determined by what we sense and experience. The whole point of knowing is that we do come into contact with reality. Her claim is that in all instances, this knowing (including knowledge held in error) is achieved through *trusting* these tacit elements. This leads Meek to conclude that *"faith is a necessary ingredient in every single act of knowing."*

Meek, *Longing To Know*, 173.

What Meek wants to convince us of is that knowing God has similar contours to any other kind of knowing (thus challenging the rejection of faith in the search for truth).

This is an invaluable correction to post-Enlightenment thought, although we also need to hold firmly to the biblical assertion that our failure in knowing God is not methodological, but moral – a point acknowledged by Meek, yet not drawn out in detail. Positively, in relation to her approach, Meek summarises: *"God meets us – in his word as our guide; in the world and in Christ; in ourselves through the Spirit's illumination. Such knowing is an integrated process as we act in faith:* 'Do you want to know God? Live his words.'"

Meek, *Longing To Know*, 140.

2. Apologetic Implications

What has been explored above are really two sides of the same coin. Both culture and what we call knowledge are public expressions of belief and worldview rooted in presuppositions. Belief is everywhere as we respond to God by doing stuff in the world and with creation, whilst everything we know, we have arrived at through a process of faith. It is against this backdrop that we contend for the truth.

Understanding the place of cultural engagement

In the sense that Edgar gives it, cultural engagement is inevitable. It relates to our being in the image of God and our being in the world: our vocation to govern and steward creation. In thinking about this, Edgar has done some incisive work, laying out a history of cultural engagement, interacting with objections, and presenting a biblical case.

In highlighting cultural engagement as a response to God, Turnau demonstrates that this stewardship of creation is not merely a human compulsion or vocation. Rather, it is connected to our understanding of reality. Edgar, Turnau, and Meek are in agreement here that our activity in the world is faith-based, meaning-orientated activity. Whilst Turnau and Edgar stress this as culture and worship (or idolatry), Meek suggests it's also an act of knowing (whether in truth or error), because: *"knowing is something we do with reality."*

Meek, *Longing To Know*, 179.

What does this mean for defending the faith?

Whilst people certainly believe and think in propositions, they don't live in them.

A gospel that connects

Given the perspective outlined here, modern culture is in many ways no different to any other 'religious' culture. And yet, crossing religious cultures to engage the unreached is held with reverence, whereas engaging with popular sub-cultures is often dismissed. Is there some discontinuity here?

Certainly, it would be a mistake to think that culture must be the starting point of every apologetic interaction. Nor is there one cultural trend that speaks for all of society. As the work of an elite minority, popular cultural narratives often appear to speak for everyone, where in reality they may not. Hence the zealous indignation when real life doesn't follow the script (#brexit #trump).

Yet it would also be a mistake to ignore the fact that an unbeliever is unavoidably immersed in a culture that constantly claims to generate meaning. The reason this is significant is that this meaning deals in concrete expressions and affections rather than abstract propositions; smuggling ideas past our brains and into our hearts. As Turnau suggests, this personally involves us and our imaginations, informing – for good or ill – what we know; creating a story that pictures the truth. In Meek's terms, such cultural works become elements of tacit knowledge.

Whilst people certainly believe and think in propositions, they don't live in them. The lives that we construct around us express a complex and nuanced web of mixed meanings related to many areas: love, death, morality, belonging, identity, redemption, relationships, and justice are all such ideas that we make sense of through the stories we create around us.

That humans grasp truth through the meaning of story is plain from Scripture. The meaning of ideas such as 'ransom,' 'redemption,' and 'propitiation' are all found throughout Scripture in the events of salvation history. Scripture helps us to grasp what the work of Christ *means* through the exodus, Passover, or return from exile narratives and the repeated retelling and re-enacting of these stories in song and festival.

This suggests that as well as broadening our idea of 'gospel opportunities,' a cultural-worldview approach encourages us to engage with unbelievers in a way that connects more personally than intellectual debate alone. That is to say, worldview apologetics works well in speaking to the affections: nobody wants a meaningless world, or morality to be arbitrary, everybody longs to be guilt free, and to find their place in a story. These are *desired* beliefs and hopes woven into the fabric of society and civilisation. With an eye to the story people are immersed in and what is meaningful to their lives, our defence of the faith is able to engage people on their heart-frequency. This is an invaluable guard against merely proclaiming Christianity as a rational proposition. Many unbelievers are more than content to be irrationally happy. We must proclaim the beauty of the truth not abstractly, but meaningfully into the lives of individuals and people groups.

Of course, we don't need a PhD in Netflix to know that the world is idolatrous. The point is that much of the Westernised world *doesn't think* it's idolatrous or religious, or that capital-T Truth is something in which we're subjectively involved. But, as Van Til reminds us, *"we cannot agree with natural man's estimate of himself."*

Van Til, *Christian Apologetics*, 123.

As an aside, it is also worth noticing the importance these issues have for connecting the gospel to *believers*. Because we're immersed in our own surrounding cultures we're immersed in the ideas of the world. As Turnau puts it, *"we are in a 'tug-of-war' for our imaginations."* His point is that viewing culture in the ways we've addressed helps develop a *"Christian-critical imagination,"* so that we resist conforming to the world, not by withdrawing, but by discerning the things that might seduce our hearts whilst our brains are looking the other way.

Turnau, *Popologetics*, 213.

ibid., 214.

Rethinking what we know

The reason Western society doesn't think it lives by faith is because of the modernist claim to objectivity. Here, Koukl's strategy is shrewd in shifting the ground of debate. As Koukl points out, in order to doubt something, one must do so on the basis of something which is not doubted. This means that any unbelieving objection is actually a truth claim, and as such requires defending. Pointing this out is a front-footed, challenging apologetic that serves our evangelism well. Biblically, we may know the unbeliever has an alternative faith, the important bit is demonstrating this to the unbeliever. In a 'post-truth' world of alternative facts, this could be a timely strategy.

Meek's work deepens this approach whilst appropriately challenging our own tradition. As Meek points out:

Meek, *Longing To Know*, 145.

Christianity has been marked by modernism... we have been blind, additionally to the misfit between our default modernist model of knowledge and Scripture.

This is a provocative reminder that the Bible doesn't present knowledge as an object to be acquired, but implores sinners to a relational knowledge of the Redeemer.

That is, the effects of sin on our minds (cf. Rom 1:24, 28).

Although Meek treads lightly on the **noetic** effect of sin, it's imperative that we don't lose sight of it in our apologetic interactions. We appeal to those who know God, being made in his image, yet reject and deny him. In doing so, we proclaim the faith that not only leads to true knowledge, but we also proclaim the knowledge that is itself the salvation they need: "This is eternal life that they may know you the only true God and Jesus Christ whom you have sent" (John 17:3).

Challenging knowledge and belief in this way offers a chance to reframe what is plausible for an unbeliever, such that the gospel is no longer branded illegitimate as a public truth claim. I think this is apologetic gold.

Not so revolutionary?

We needn't see this approach, however, as anything revolutionary or overly complicated (after all, Meek's proposal recalls Anselm – via Augustine: *"I believe in order to understand"*). In addition, appealing to the gospel as a better story in the face of objection is something we often do intuitively (think of how we might engage objection in current gender debates by returning to Genesis and re-narrating the story of what it is to be human). Perhaps the greatest benefit in approaching apologetics this way is that we defend and proclaim Christ crucified, rather than the probability of theism, or logically infer the existence of a creator. Might this be closer to the way the New Testament presents an *apologia* for the good news of the ascended Lord Jesus?

In Conclusion

Teasing out the reliance on ultimate commitments and the inconsistency of the non-Christian worldview exposes the fallacy of objectivity and credibly asserts belief as a public necessity. The 'madman' making a public case for belief and questioning the facts is not as mad as he first appears. On the contrary, an insistence on 'brute facts' and an attempt to discern truth from a godless premise suggests a more questionable outlook. How then might we take more opportunity to show this is the case?

Apologetically, there's great value in demonstrating that society doesn't live in logical consistency with 'the facts' that we all agree on. Moreover, there's perhaps even greater value in demonstrating how our search for meaning is only truly fulfilled in Christ. This defence is not a generic deism, but the panoramic good news revealed to us in all of Scripture that speaks to all of life. This truth is not only right, it is glorious, attractive and fulfilling. Christ came, not that we would have mere intellectual understanding, but that we might have life, and life to the full. We could do much worse than defending the hope of this life in the fullest possible way.

This is an apologetic approach that presents an opportunity to take every thought captive for Christ – whether challenging a secular creed, crossing sub-cultures, or even chatting about that interview with the bloke from *Carpool Karaoke*.

Questions for further thought and discussion

1. Leslie Newbigin warned that *"what is really being asked is that we should show that the gospel is in accordance with the reigning plausibility structure of our society, that it accords with the assumptions which we normally do not doubt; and that is exactly what we cannot and must not do."*

   Lesslie Newbigin, *Truth to Tell: The Gospel as Public Truth* (London: SPCK, 1991), 28.

   Why does Matt agree? Do you?

2. Why does Bill Edgar think it's so important to interpret culture through a religious lens?

3. How does Esther Meek's work break down the idea that faith and facts have nothing to do with each other?

4. Ted Turnau argues that *"popular-cultural works form 'worlds of meaning' for us to inhabit."* What examples can you think of and how do they reflect or distort the reality of God's creation? Where do you recognise the tug-of-war for your own imagination?

AN INFINITY OF INFINITELY HAPPY LIFE

An excerpt from Blaise Pascal's
Pensées with commentary

Blaise Pascal (1623-1662) is no doubt the most original Christian apologist of the modern era. He was a scientist and mathematician, doing pioneering work on barometric pressure, probability theory and the vacuum. But his enduring renown is for his writings on matters of theology.

WILLIAM EDGAR is Professor of Apologetics at Westminster Theological Seminary, Philadelphia. His scholarly interests include apologetics, theology, aesthetics, African-American music, and ethics. For fun he enjoys jazz piano and Brazilian soccer.

His *Provincial Letters* (1656-57) were a compelling defence of sovereign grace, and a scathing indictment of the moral laxity of the church. The elegant French and the cogency of his arguments won him the acclaim of many, including Voltaire and Jean-Jacques Rousseau. It also got him a condemnation from Pope Alexander VII, who nevertheless soon thereafter enacted sweeping reforms in the church. Pascal's written style was full of learning and a great sense of irony, which has led historians to recognise that he had a hand in modernising the French language.

It was his masterpiece, *Les Pensées*, however, which gained him a permanent place in the defenders-of-the-faith hall of fame. It was intended to be an apologetic for the Christian faith and is composed of a series of numbered 'thoughts' (*pensées* is French for 'thoughts'). Some are lengthy, others pithy; some are downright cryptic, as though they were notes to self. While there is some debate about the order of these thoughts, there is no doubt about the themes that link them together: the misery of the human soul without grace, the judgment of God, and his mercy through Jesus Christ.

Pascal wrote at the dawn of the European Enlightenment. During this time the authority of the church, and of the Bible, were being put into question. It was increasingly believed that human reason was fully capable of understanding the way the world works, and the place of mankind within the world. As the role of reason became more and more prominent, many, including Pascal, began to worry that unaided reason would beget, not freedom, but spiritual dangers. Pascal is thus situated at a crucial crossroads in Western history.

We know most about his life from the account of his adoring sister Gilberte. He never had a proper childhood, because he was nearly always a sickly young man, but at a young age could be found studying Greek, Latin, mathematics and geometry. Early on, he wrote a powerful text about suffering, one that asked God to help him make good use of his illnesses.

Three incidents sealed his own entry into the Christian faith (1654). (1) On a leisurely outing the horses driving his carriage plunged into the Seine on the Pont de Neuilly. It stopped abruptly before he would have been plunged to his death. He was sure God was sparing him for a few more years. (2) His niece, Marguerite, was miraculously healed of an eye infection which had been deemed incurable by the doctors. Pascal was sure it was God, through his Son Jesus Christ who effected her cure. (3) In November Pascal experienced a night full of the palpable sense that God was visiting him. He wrote a *memorial* which he kept inside the lining of his jacket, which read,

"

Year of grace 1654, Monday 23 November, feast of St. Clement... from about half past ten at night to about half an hour after midnight, FIRE. God of Abraham, God of Isaac, God of Jacob, not of philosophers and scholars. Certitude, heartfelt joy, peace. God of Jesus Christ. God of Jesus Christ. "My God and your God"... Joy, Joy, Joy, tears of joy... Jesus Christ. Jesus Christ. May I never be separated from him.

He spent the rest of his life praying, writing, and encouraging his other sister Jacqueline's community, the Jansenists, followers of the Dutch Augustinian Cornelius Jansen. Pascal died at 39 of multiple ailments.

In the following passages, we discover the way Pascal conceived of the role of reason as it relates to faith. Pascal was not opposed to reason, but to *rationalism*, the claim that reason is all-sufficient. He puts his views succinctly in #183: *"Two excesses: to exclude reason, to admit nothing but reason."* It would be important to look at the entire body of his writings in order to discern the full picture, but we get a good sense of it here. Then, we will encounter an argument for which he has become celebrated, *The Wager*. A fair examination of this argument will reveal some of its subtleties, as well as its persuasive power.

Excerpt taken from Blaise Pascal, *Pensées*, translated by A. J. Krailsheimer (London: Penguin Classics, 1995) 53-57, 121-27. Reproduced by permission of Penguin Books Ltd.

167 Submission and use of reason; that is what makes true Christianity.

168 How I hate such foolishness as not believing in the Eucharist, etc. If the Gospel is true, if Jesus Christ is God, where is the difficulty?

In the Pensées Pascal spends a good deal of time discussing the place of reason in relation to faith. While he believed the Christian faith was reasonable, he did not submit that faith to unaided autonomous reason.

Throughout his writings he pleads that there be no conflict between the use of reason and accepting invisible realities.

169 I should not be a Christian but for the miracles, says St Augustine.

170 *Submission.* One must know when it is right to doubt, to affirm, to submit. Anyone who does otherwise does not understand the force of reason. Some men run counter to these principles, either affirming that everything can be proved, because they know nothing about proof, or doubting everything, because they do not know when to submit, or always submitting, because they do not know when judgment is called for.

Sceptic, mathematician, Christian, doubt, affirmation, submission.

Clearly Pascal understood that reason should admit to norms and not pretend to be self-sufficient.

Lines like this reflect the way the Pensées are Pascal's fragmentary notebooks. In a few places, like this, he has just jotted down words or small phrases.

171 *They received the word with all readiness of mind, and searched the Scriptures daily, whether those things were so.*

Quoted from Acts 17:11, which praises the Bereans for testing what they heard with Scripture. Italics in our text are used for titles, but also to indicate where Pascal used languages other than French.

172 The way of God, who disposes all things with gentleness, is to instil religion into our minds with reasoned arguments, and into our hearts with grace, but attempting to instil it into hearts and minds with force and threats is to instil not religion but terror. *Terror rather than religion.*

173 If we submit everything to reason our religion will be left with nothing mysterious or supernatural.

If we offend the principles of reason our religion will be absurd and ridiculous.

174 St Augustine. Reason would never submit unless it judged that there are occasions when it ought to submit.

See Augustine, *Letters*, 122.5.

It is right, then, that reason should submit when it judges that it ought to submit.

175 One of the ways in which the damned will be confounded is that they will see themselves condemned by their own reason, by which they claimed to condemn the Christian religion.

176 Those who do not love truth excuse themselves on the grounds that it is disputed and that very many people deny it. Thus their error is solely due to the fact that they love neither truth nor charity, and so they have no excuse.

177 Contradiction is a poor indication of truth.
   Many things that are certain are contradicted.
   Many that are false pass without contradiction.
   Contradiction is no more an indication of falsehood than lack of it is an indication of truth.

178 See the two sorts of men under the title: *Perpetuity*. (286)

179 There are few true Christians. I mean even as regards faith. There are plenty who believe, but out of superstition. There are plenty who do not believe, but because they are libertines; there are few in between.
   I do not include those who lead a really devout life, nor all those who believe by intuition of the heart.

180 Jesus Christ performed miracles, and then the apostles, and the early saints in great numbers, because, since the prophecies were not yet fulfilled, and were being fulfilled by them, there was no witness save that of their miracles. It was foretold that the Messiah would convert the nations. How could this prophecy be fulfilled without the conversion of the nations, and how could the nations be converted to the Messiah when they could not see the final effect of the prophecies which prove him? Therefore, until he had died, risen again, and converted the nations, all things were not fulfilled and so miracles were needed throughout this time. Now there is no more need of miracles against the Jews, for the fulfilment of the prophecies is a continuing miracle.

181 Piety is different from superstition
   To carry piety to the point of superstition is to destroy it.
   Heretics reproach us for superstitious submission, and that is doing what they reproach us for.
   Impiety of not believing in the Eucharist because it cannot be seen.
   Superstition of believing certain propositions.
   Faith, etc.

182 There is nothing so consistent with reason as this denial of reason.

183 Two excesses: to exclude reason, to admit nothing but reason.

184 It would have been no sin not to believe Jesus Christ without miracles.
   Look upon me... if I lie.   Job 6:28

185 Faith certainly tells us what the senses do not, but not the contrary of what they see; it is above, not against them.

This kind of statement confirms Pascal's acceptance of visible proofs.

186 You abuse the trust people have in the Church and make them believe anything.

187 There is nothing unusual in having to reproach people for being too docile. It is a vice as natural as incredulity and just as pernicious.
   Superstition.

188 Reason's last step is the recognition that there are an infinite number of things which are beyond it. It is merely feeble if it does not go as far as to realize that.
   If natural things are beyond it, what are we to say about supernatural things?

XIV • EXCELLENCE OF THIS MEANS OF PROVING GOD

189 *God through Jesus Christ.* We know God only through Jesus Christ. Without this mediator all communication with God is broken off. Through Jesus we know God. All those who have claimed to know God and prove his existence without Jesus Christ have only had futile proofs to offer. But to prove Christ we have the prophecies which are solid and palpable proofs. By being fulfilled and true by the event, these prophecies show that these truths are certain and thus prove that Jesus is divine. In him and through him, therefore, we know God. Apart from that, without Scripture, without original sin, without the necessary mediator, who was promised and came, it is impossible to prove absolutely that God exists, or to teach sound doctrine and sound morality. But through and in Christ we can prove God's existence, and teach both doctrine and morality. Therefore Jesus is the true God of men.

But at the same time we know our own wretchedness, because this God is nothing less than our redeemer from wretchedness. Thus we can know God properly only by knowing our own iniquities.

Those who have known God without knowing their own wretchedness have not glorified him but themselves.

1 Corinthians 1:21

For after that... the world by wisdom knew not God, it pleased God by the foolishness of preaching to save them that believe.

190 *Preface.* The metaphysical proofs for the existence of God are so remote from human reasoning and so involved that they make little impact, and, even if they did help some people, it would only be for the moment during which they watched the demonstration, because an hour later they would be afraid they had made a mistake.

Augustine, *Sermons*, 112.

What they gained by curiosity they lost through pride.

That is the result of knowing God without Christ, in other words communicating without a mediator with a God known without a mediator.

Whereas those who have known God through a mediator know their own wretchedness.

191 It is not only impossible but useless to know God without Christ. They are drawn closer to him, not further away. They are not humbled... but *The better*

Bernard, *Sermons on the Song of Songs*, 84.

one is the worse one becomes if one attributes this excellence to oneself.

192 Knowing God without knowing our own wretchedness makes for pride. Knowing our own wretchedness without knowing God makes for despair. Knowing Jesus Christ strikes the balance because he shows us both God and our own wretchedness.

This is one of the most powerful statements in the Pensées.

UNCLASSIFIED PAPERS: SERIES II (THE WAGER)

418 *Infinity – nothing.* Our soul is cast into the body where it finds numbers, time, dimensions; it reasons about these things and calls them natural, or necessary, and can believe nothing else.

Unity added to infinity does not increase it at all, any more than a foot added to an infinite measurement: the finite is annihilated in the presence of the infinite and becomes pure nothingness. So it is with our mind before God, with our justice before divine justice. There is not so great a disproportion between our justice and God's as between unity and infinity.

God's justice must be as vast as his mercy. Now his justice towards the damned is less vast and ought to be less startling to us than his mercy toward the elect.

We know that the infinite exists without knowing its nature, just as we know that it is untrue that numbers are finite. Thus it is true that there is an infinite number, but we do not know what it is. It is untrue that it is even, untrue that it is odd, for by adding a unit it does not change its nature. Yet it is a number, and every number is even or odd. (It is true that this applies to every finite number.)

Therefore we may know that God exists without knowing what he is.

Is there no substantial truth, seeing that there are so many true things which are not truth itself?

Thus we know the existence and nature of the finite because we too are finite and extended in space.

We know the existence of the infinite without knowing its nature, because it too has extension but unlike us no limits.

But we do not know either the existence or the nature of God, because he has neither extension nor limits.

But by faith we know his existence, through glory we shall know his nature.

Now I have already proved that it is quite possible to know that something exists without knowing its nature.

Let us now speak according to our natural lights.

If there is God, he is infinitely beyond our comprehension, since, being invisible and without limits, he bears no relation to us. We are therefore incapable of knowing either what he is or whether he is. That being so, who would dare to attempt an answer to the question? Certainly not we, who bear no relation to him.

Who then will condemn Christians for being unable to give rational grounds for their belief, professing as they do a religion for which they cannot give rational grounds? They declare that it is a folly, *stultitiam*, in expounding it to the world, and then you complain that they do not prove it. If they did prove it they would not be keeping their word. It is by being without proof that they show they are not without sense. 'Yes, but although that excuses those who offer their religion as such, and absolves them from the criticism of producing it without rational grounds, it does not absolve those who accept it.' Let us then examine this point, and let us say: 'Either God is or he is not.' But to which view shall we be inclined? Reason cannot decide this question. Infinite chaos separates us. At the far end of this infinite distance a coin is being spun which will come down heads or tails. How will you wager? Reason cannot make you choose either, reason cannot prove either wrong.

Do not then condemn as wrong those who have made a choice, for you know nothing about it. 'No, but I will condemn them not for having made this particular choice, but any choice, for, although the one who calls heads and the other one are equally at fault, the fact is that they are both at fault: the right thing is not to wager at all.'

Yes, but you must wager. There is no choice, you are already committed. Which will you choose, then? Let us see: since a choice must be made, let us see which offers you the least interest. You have two things to lose: the true and the good; and two things to stake: your reason and your will, your knowledge and your happiness; and your nature has two things to avoid: error and wretchedness. Since you must necessarily choose, your reason is no more affronted by choosing one rather than the other. That is one point cleared up. But your happiness? Let us weigh up the gain and the loss involved in calling heads that God exists. Let us assess the two cases: if you win you win everything, if you lose you lose nothing. Do not hesitate then; wager that he does exist. 'That is wonderful. Yes, I must wager, but perhaps I am wagering too much.' Let us see: since there is an equal chance of gain and loss, if you stood to win only two lives for one you would still wager, but supposing you stood to win three?

These rather involved thoughts are crucial in order to understand what follows: the argument known as the wager. One cannot reduce God to a finite entity. The 'wager' is not an empirical proof. Accordingly, what follows is not proclaimed with the authority of Scripture.

"Foolishness". See 1 Corinthians 1:18.

The premise of the wager is that we not only must chose, but we have already chosen. Refusing to make the right choice is in fact a wrong choice. Reason alone cannot make such a decision. It must be made by weighing the high stakes. If God exists, and you take the step of faith to believe in him, then you have gained an infinitely happy life. If you believe in him and he does not exist, you have at least gained a fruitful life here on earth. If you refuse to believe him and he does exist you have made a fatal error. For Pascal this is not simply a business calculation but a moral investment: refusal to believe is foolish, driven by sinful passions.

You would have to play (since you must necessarily play) and it would be unwise of you, once you are obliged to play, not to risk your life in order to win three lives at a game in which there is an equal chance of losing and winning. But there is an eternity of life and happiness. That being so, even though there were an infinite number of chances, of which only one were in your favour, you would still be right to wager one in order to win two; and you would be acting wrongly, being obliged to play, in refusing to stake one life against three in a game, where out of an infinite number of chances there is one in your favour, if there were an infinity of infinitely happy life to be won. But here there is an infinity of infinitely happy life to be won, one chance of winning against a finite number of chances of losing, and what you are staking is finite. That leaves no choice; wherever there is infinity, and where there are not infinite chances of losing against that of winning, there is no room for hesitation, you must give everything. And thus, since you are obliged to play, you must be renouncing reason if you hoard your life rather than risk it for an infinite gain, just as likely to occur as a loss amounting to nothing.

For it is no good saying that it is uncertain whether you will win, that it is certain that you are taking a risk, and that the infinite distance between the certainty of what you are risking and the uncertainty of what you may gain makes the finite good you are certainly risking equal to the infinite good that you are not certain to gain. This is not the case. Every gambler takes a certain risk for an uncertain gain, and yet he is taking a certain finite risk for an uncertain finite gain without sinning against reason...

Again, what may appear to some to be a cold business calculation is meant rather to be an impassioned plea for a soulful decision.

End of this address

'Now what harm will come to you from choosing this course? You will be faithful, honest, humble, grateful, full of good works, a sincere, true friend... It is true you will not enjoy noxious pleasures, glory and good living, but will you not have others?

'I tell you that you will gain in this life, and that at every step you take along this road you will see that your gain is so certain and your risk so negligible that in the end you will realize that you have wagered on something certain and infinite for which you have paid nothing.'

'How these words fill me with rapture and delight! –'

Not only the emotional content but the commitment to prayer and piety are striking in what could have been an abstract philosophical discussion.

'If my words please you and seem cogent, you must know that they come from a man who went down upon his knees before and after to pray this infinite and indivisible being, to whom he submits his own, that he might bring your being also to submit to him for your own good and for his glory: and that strength might thus be reconciled with lowliness.'

——— EXCERPT ENDS ———

CONCLUSION

The contrast between Montaigne, Descartes and Pascal could not be greater. Montaigne, for all his wisdom, plunges us into ignorance. Descartes says that mankind has been caught in childish immaturity, but that if he will trust in his reason he will find freedom. Pascal taught that humanity is lost in its pretensions and that its vanity keeps it from knowing God. If only we would take the bold step of commitment, believing that God, through Jesus Christ, can save us and bring us to a child-like faith, then only can we find freedom. It is safe to say that Descartes' vision, occasionally tempered by the irrational scepticism of Montaigne, has given birth to the modern mind. We still seem to share the Enlightenment spirit, and its confidence in the power of mankind to triumph over its infantile dependence on religion and other superstitions. If we are disillusioned by the spirit of Descartes, we fall into the meaninglessness of Montaigne's.

Pascal invites us to look with proper fear and trembling at a sovereign God who will judge the living and the dead. When we do we will be confronted with our misery. But we will find that he gently invites us to abandon our misguided trust in our own abilities and to turn to the one who can give us our true identity. And we can know him with certainty. The choice is between the god of the philosophers and the God of Abraham, Isaac and Jacob. There is the 'fire' needed to purge us of evil and renew us in the Lord's loving arms. Today, that choice has never been more urgent.

Questions for further thought and discussion

1. *"Two excesses: to exclude reason, to admit nothing but reason."*

   Why was that such an important point for Pascal, and how does it fit with what Matt Peckham argued in his article?

2. Pascal made much of an appeal to happiness. He wrote elsewhere in the Pensées that,

   All men seek happiness. This is without exception. Whatever different means they employ, they all tend to this end. The cause of some going to war, and of others avoiding it, is the same desire in both, attended with different views. This is the motive of every action of every man, even of those who hang themselves.

   How does this extract reflect that interest in happiness? And what are the strengths and weaknesses of appealing to people's desire for happiness?

3. Why does Pascal insist that Jesus has to be at the centre of apologetics? How does that fit with the rest of this issue of *Primer*?

CHURCHES! TIME MACHINES! A GOSPEL APOLOGETIC!

JONATHAN LEEMAN PRESENTS

WE COME IN PEACE!

Imagine thousands, even tens of thousands, of alien ships suddenly appearing around the globe. Government officials and police forces cautiously move in. News channels carry the images to stunned faces in restaurants, offices, and homes.

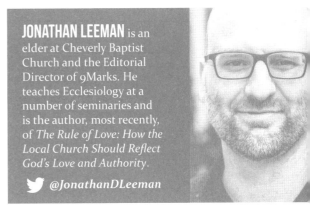

JONATHAN LEEMAN is an elder at Cheverly Baptist Church and the Editorial Director of 9Marks. He teaches Ecclesiology at a number of seminaries and is the author, most recently, of *The Rule of Love: How the Local Church Should Reflect God's Love and Authority*.

@JonathanDLeeman

Yet the doors of the ships open, and ordinary men and women walk out. They speak the language of whatever country they land in. They wear the clothes of those countries. "We're not from another planet," they say. "We're from the earth's future. We represent a day when one kingdom will cover the whole planet, like the waters cover the sea."

The ships are not alien spacecraft but time machines.

Their message about a planet-sized kingdom sounds both far-fetched and menacing. Once a week they will gather at their time machines for further instruction and for rehearsing the message of this coming kingdom through song and prayer. But they explain that they mean no harm. They will live among us peacefully and quietly. "And you're welcome to join us!" they cheerfully add.

These citizens of a future kingdom have come, they continue, to share a message about the love and judgment of their king and to demonstrate that message with their lives. They claim we have offended their king and that we need to be reconciled to him. Apparently, he lived on our planet a couple of thousand years ago and was an incarnation of God himself. Then he died to pay the penalty for wrongdoing and rose from the grave.

It's a strange message, to be sure. Yet as weeks, then months, then years pass, we have the opportunity to watch these folks live out their message. What does it look like when it's lived out?

From our perspective, some things are attractive, other things are offensive.

They commit to each other and watch over each other. They love and make sacrifices for each other. They don't kill their babies or their elderly. They work at caring for their spouses and children through ups and downs. They don't just care for one another's needs, but the needs of our people. They share their goods. They pursue justice for the oppressed and comfort for the hurting. They practice business in a way that benefits every party, not just themselves, nor depends on maintaining a permanent underclass. They are continual learners, reading their Book and books about their Book.

All that's good, but the good comes with an underbelly of criticism toward us and our world. No, we cannot kill our babies. No, we cannot sleep with whomever we want. No, we cannot define ourselves, our gender, or our plans willy-nilly. No, we cannot offer bribes or fiddle the books or skimp on taxes or exploit every advantage for personal gain. Yes, we have to give. Yes, we have to obey the law. Yes, we have to be patient with the hurting. Yes, we have to apologise for wrongdoing and admit that we're self-centred and give all that up. Perhaps most offensively of all, they propose that we become one of *them*, citizens of the future.

Who do they think they are? It's presumptuous, arrogant, ignorant, exclusivist, intolerant!

They say they're not revolutionaries. They don't want to overthrow the government or topple the markets. But the way they live – and by example call us to live – could undermine our governments and markets. Certainly, whole industries would crumble if we lived like them. And many governments would have to change their way of doing business.

They're a funny people, to say the least. They're nice on the surface, but they don't live and let live. There's an edge to everything they do. An agenda. They both love and condemn, hug and hit, you might say. There's something right and humane about them, admittedly, but there's something obnoxious and threatening, too. At best, these people are weird.

THE CHURCH IS A TIME MACHINE

Hopefully, the connections I want to make are obvious. Local churches – your congregation and mine – are those time machines. The gospel of Jesus Christ and the power of the Holy Spirit have broken into history and established them as embassies of the end times. The rule of Christ will be universally and fully visible at the end of the age. Yet local churches offer glimpses of Christ's rule now locally. The life and structures and fellowship of particular congregations are the *already* in the *already*/*not yet* of **inaugurated eschatology**.

That is, the thought that the new creation has already broken into the present age. For more on this, see Stephen Witmer's article in *Primer* issue 05.

Churches possess an ambassadorial message: "be reconciled to God" (2 Cor 5:20). And that message should be matched by a counter-cultural community: "go out from their midst, and be separate from them... bringing holiness to completion" (2 Cor 6:17, 7:1).

What I'd like to emphasise in this piece is the apologetic role the life of a church plays in giving credit to our message. The most powerful apologetic for the gospel, the thing that gives credit to the evangelistic message once it's spoken, will generally not be a philosophical argument, whether evidentialist or presuppositionalist. It will be the loving and holy life of a people in community, a church:

John 13:34-35

> *A new commandment I give to you, that you love one another: just as I have loved you, you also are to love one another. By this all people will know that you are my disciples, if you have love for one another.*

People will recognise our membership in Christ not by our love for them, says the verse, but by our love for one another.

Want to convince unbelievers that our views on sexuality are not bigoted and intolerant? It's not just the clever articles we write that will convince them. It will be flourishing adolescents, singles, and marriages, where those who stumble into this or that temptation find themselves meaningfully embraced by a new-creation family.

Want to convince them that what the Bible says about male leadership in home and church is not oppressive? Write books on this topic, sure, but, more than that, consider what it takes to cultivate a culture of happy, strong, and engaged women.

Want to undermine the claim that Christians don't care about justice? Then preach the word, all of it, and cultivate a culture of discipling and good deeds, where congregations present a picture of true justice and righteousness, both within themselves and spilling outward.

Even with all of this, some people will hate what they see. Living by the law of God contradicts the law of fallen hearts. Therefore, they will "insult you, persecute you and falsely say all kinds of evil against you because of me" (Matt 5:11).

Yet as they revile they will experience an inner dissonance. Their natures were designed by God, and they were made to prosper best when living by his law. Something inside of them will testify against their reviling (see Rom 1:20-21). And then some, wonderfully, will be drawn to what they observe. They will "see your good deeds and glorify your Father in heaven" (Matt 5:16).

The point in all of this is that we, the saints, must be distinct – like salt. What good is salt if it loses its saltiness? You might as well throw it out (Matt 5:13). It's ironic, then, that so many books and conferences for church leaders emphasise the topic of relevance, as if our challenge is showing the world that we're like them. In fact, the main challenge for churches today is the same challenge God's people have experienced ever since wandering in the wilderness: not being like the nations, but being distinct from them.

The relationship between our *message* and our *life* looks like this:

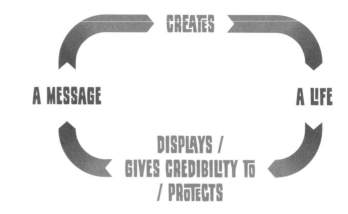

A message creates a life. And that life in turn displays the message, gives credibility to the message, protects the message. In short, it acts as an apologetic or defence for the message.

Churches need – the nations need – messages and lives from the future. We all need a glimpse of what *will be* based on *what we are* based on what Christ *has done*.

Speaking of what Christ has done, we need to use more specific words than the generic "message" and "life." The Bible locates the dynamic interplay we just observed between message and life in the relationship between the gospel message and the local community of believers we call a church, like this:

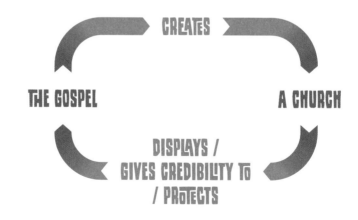

The gospel creates a church. And a church displays, gives credibility to, and protects the gospel. People can become Christians apart from the church, but apart from the church they will have difficulty displaying and giving credibility to the gospel message. They will have difficulty protecting the message in their own life or in the lives of others.

Think of all those people who call themselves Christians because they heard and embraced the gospel message, but who try to live the Christian life apart from membership in a local church. They *might* be Christians. But at best they're ineffective Christians. They don't present an attractive witness in their workplace or homes. Their lives are slightly cleaned up versions of non-Christian lives. Therefore, their children don't follow them into Christianity, nor do their friends. The gospel's witness is unprotected. It's not durable. It lasts maybe one generation.

For instance, I think of my friend Jared (not his real name). He calls himself a Christian. He can give an orthodox explanation of the faith. But he's reluctant to bind himself to any one church. Instead, he plans meals and coffees with a number of Christian friends from different churches, most of whom are his age and share his socio-economic status and political opinions. Generally, they reinforce Jared's opinions of himself, partly because he refuses to hear otherwise. And little by little I've been watching Jared adopt unorthodox views of Scripture in order to support his preferred sexual lifestyle. If Jared really is a Christian – and I'm not sure that he is – he's radically undermining the gospel's would-be impact on his life and in the lives of others. He certainly is not extending the gospel's reach by making disciples.

Jesus gave us churches, among other things, to preserve the gospel and to make it shine. Churches are like the gold prongs of an engagement ring, Mark Dever has said. They hold the diamond of the gospel in place. Imagine instead a man who gives an unattached diamond to his fiancée, and then she keeps the diamond in her pockets. Eventually that diamond will fall through a hole or end up in the laundry. So it is among those who are wise-in-their-own-eyes and try to live the gospel outside a church.

Yet the connection between the gospel and a church is not merely a pragmatic one. Christians shouldn't join churches simply because it's good for us. We join churches because that's what we *are* – members of the body of Christ. Peter says, "Once you were not a people, but now you are God's people; once you had not received mercy, but now you have received mercy" (1 Pet 2:10). Notice that receiving God's mercy – becoming a Christian – happens simultaneously with becoming God's people.

Justifying church involvement principally on a pragmatic basis runs deep among Protestants. John Calvin, for instance, begins the very first paragraph of his book on the church this way. We gain Christ by faith, he says in the first sentence. The second sentence follows: "Since, however, in our ignorance and sloth…we need outward helps to beget and increase faith within us, and advance it to its goal, God has also added these aids that he may provide for our weakness." And these aids are preaching, the sacraments, pastors and teachers, the church, and its governance. In other words, he encourages us to unite ourselves to churches for the pragmatic good that they will do. John Calvin, Institutes of the Christian Religion, ed. John T. McNeill; trans. Ford Lewis Battles; 2 vols (Philadelphia: Westminster, 1960), IV.i.1 (Battles 2:1011-12).

Or think of the two 'buts' in Ephesians 2. First is the "But God" pointing to our vertical reconciliation with Christ, where God raises us up and seats us in the heavenly places (2:1-10). Second is the "But now in Christ Jesus" pointing to the horizontal reconciliation between Jew and Gentile, where those who were far off are brought near and become one new man (2:11-22). Being covenantally united to God means being covenantally united to God's people. Horizontal reconciliation necessarily follows the vertical. Mom and dad adopt me from the orphanage then bring me home where I discover new brothers and sisters.

In short, the gospel does not just create individual Christians. It creates a community, a family, a body. The gospel is church-shaped.

And don't miss how concrete that community must be. The gospel doesn't merely create a vague "warm thoughts toward our worldwide brotherhood" community. It creates a concrete covenanted-together, geographically-located, accountability-providing list of actual names that we call a local church. Hey look, there's brother Bob, sister Sue, and deacon Dev. We don't get to choose our fellow church members or their problems like we get to choose our friends. Rather, we're stuck with whoever joins the church, like brothers and sisters at the dinner table. Joining or covenanting with a local church is how we "put on" our membership in the new covenant body of Christ, just like we "put on" our covenantal righteousness in Christ by pursuing righteousness. Don't tell me you're righteous in Christ if you're not pursuing a life of righteousness. Likewise, don't tell me you belong to the family of God if you're not showing up at the family dinner table. I need to know your name, and you need to know mine, in order for us to keep each other accountable in the gospel.

In other words, the gospel doesn't just create the Church – capital C. It creates churches – small c. It comes into your life and mine and gives us a *new identity* (son, brother, sister) and makes *new demands*. Formally speaking, the gospel demands that we wear the Jesus nametag on our lapels (so to speak) by being baptised into his name (Matt 28:19). The gospel requires us to gather with other believers in his name so that we might jointly exercise the keys of the kingdom, that is, affirm publicly the *what* and the *who* of the gospel, confessions and confessors (Matt 16:13-20; 18:15-20). It demands that we gather regularly together, both to affirm one another as one body as we partake of the one bread as well as to spur one another on to love and good deeds (1 Cor 10:17; Heb 10:25). It requires us to submit to our leaders as men who will give an account (Heb 13:17). Informally, the gospel demands that we love and care and correct and feed and give and warn and disciple and evangelise and abide as a family throughout the week.

So *become* what you *are* by joining a church. You are no longer just an "I." God has made you a "we."

In other words, the gospel possesses an intrinsic social dynamic, and that dynamic is the local church. A local church is a presentation of the gospel, a picture of the gospel, the outworking of the gospel, the gospel on display. And in all of these ways it works as an apologetic for the gospel.

I think of Ryan, an atheist, who grew up with Christian friends in Texas. He partied with them on Friday and Saturday nights, but then watched them attend church on Sunday mornings. Their hypocrisy turned him off from Christianity. Then after college in Washington DC, his family entered a series of crises. My church first cared for his mother, who became a Christian. Then it cared for him and his twin brother, who followed their mother into salvation. What struck Ryan, according to his testimony, was how well the church had cared for his mother as well as how the members looked after each other. It was dramatically different than the churches he had witnessed as a youth. The life of the church served as an apologetic for the message it proclaimed.

JUSTIFICATION AND JUSTICE

What is the gospel? It is the good news that Jesus paid the penalty for sinners, rose again, declares righteous all who repent and believe, and is now remaking this faith-filled people in his own image, to be revealed fully at the end of history. I can share this gospel with you on an aeroplane, never see you again, and you can be saved if you only repent and believe, like the thief on the cross.

Yet, once again, we cannot miss how profoundly social, even political, this gospel is. The gospel of justification by faith alone in Christ alone creates a whole new body politic, one where a true justice and righteousness finally prevail. And the just, righteous lives of these people in turn protect and testify to the message of justification by faith alone. Like this:

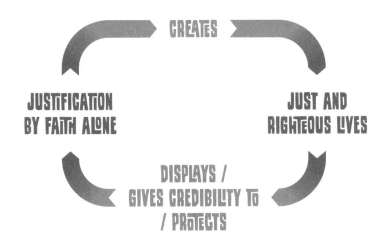

CREATES

JUSTIFICATION BY FAITH ALONE

JUST AND RIGHTEOUS LIVES

DISPLAYS / GIVES CREDIBILITY TO / PROTECTS

How? First, God's courtroom declaration "righteous" renders us righteous not just before his throne, but before all the citizens of his kingdom. It's like a judge's verdict of "not guilty." That verdict makes a person innocent before the judge, yes, but also before the bailiff, the sheriff, the courtroom clerk, the courtroom audience, indeed, the whole town. So, too, God's *forensic* declaration, by its very nature, is a *political* declaration. It creates a whole new body politic. Each individual declaration – "You're righteous"; "You're righteous"; "You're righteous" – reinstates a free citizen of God's kingdom with all the rights and privileges thereof (see Gal 4:1-7), and every member of that body politic now possesses equal standing before the throne. "And no longer shall each one teach his neighbour and each his brother, saying, 'Know the Lord,' for they shall all know me, from the least of them to the greatest, declares the Lord." (Jer 31:34a)

Second, justification by faith alone means the end of self-justification, and self-justification is the throne upon which all self-rule sits. Self-justification is an argument that says, "I deserve to rule *because* I'm wiser than God" or "wealthier than them" or "whiter than you." Self-justification is the argument underneath all tyranny, oppression, exploitation, abuse, sin. Paul offers an illustration with the Jews of his day: to those who "rely on the law" and regard themselves as virtuous, he challenges, "While you preach against stealing, do you steal? You who say that one must not commit adultery, do you commit adultery? You who abhor idols, do you rob temples?" (Rom 2:21b-22). Their self-justification yielded self-rule or sin.

Paul's solution? We must seek "the righteousness of God through faith in Jesus Christ for all who believe" (Rom 3:22). If you kill self-justification, you kill the argument *for* self-rule and *against* God's rule. Blessed are the poor in spirit, and blessed are those who have closed their mouths (Rom 3:19) and stopped boasting (Rom 3:27). Justification by faith alone, in other words, may well be the most powerful political doctrine in the Bible. If self-rule sits on the throne of self-justification, God's rule sits on the throne of God's justification. Christ's vicarious righteousness relieves us of our need to prove ourselves and the superiority of our works, our class, our skin colour, our nationality, our Sunday School attendance, our wealth, our family name, or the thousands of other things we use to justify ourselves and lord it over one another. It puts the trophy in our hands – all the privileges of Christ's covenant – so that we no longer have to win it with a sword, and that sword can now be beaten into a ploughshare, the spear into a pruning hook. Our status as equals with one another and our voting-rights as citizens of Christ's kingdom depend upon Christ's merit not our own. We have nothing to boast about. Rather, we are free to promote one another's good for Christ's sake. The community of Christ's people, then, are those who acknowledge that God rules and that their citizenship status depends on mercy. They can practice the first-fruits of true justice and righteousness, as will be revealed in the final judgment.

See Rom 2:6-7,13; 8:1,13; 14:10-12; 1 Cor 4:4-5; 2 Cor. 5:10; Gal 5:21; 6:8.

They can do this, third, because God has granted them his Spirit. His law now rests within their hearts (Jer 31:33; Ezek 36:27). The vicariously and covenantally justified community becomes the just community. And the justice of that community witnesses to its message of justification. What does this look like? Typically, it doesn't look like the stuff of television biopics, as with a BBC or PBS special on William Wilberforce. The pursuit of justice among church members might occasionally rise to such heights, but ordinarily their righteous activities will be quieter, more common. Member Mark quietly slips money into member Ethel's mailbox. Members Joe and Janet invite member Alan, who has decided to live as a life-long celibate because of the strength of his same-sex attraction, to live with them and be a part of their family. Member Gina, who is white, confesses her racism to member Dan, who is black, and finds forgiveness. Philip's Bible study of young single men, all members, spend Friday night in the nursing home with member Helen, who can no longer make it to church. Remember, they will know we are his disciples by our love for one another. But, also, a small group considers how they might care for the refugees placed by the government in their neighbourhood. And another small group works together in a crisis pregnancy centre. We seek to do good to all people.

In the previous section I offered the challenge to stop saying you're a family member if you never show up at the family dinner table. By the same token, you should stop calling yourself a Christian if you give little attention to justice and righteousness. If the church is a time machine from the future, the just and righteous activities of the saints are the very things that differentiate the citizens of the future from the ordinary citizens of today. Justice and righteousness is our culture, our accent, our style.

At the end of history, Christ's rule over the entire cosmos will be fully revealed. Yet that rule is becoming apparent in our love and righteousness now. Our life and message matter when we gather and when we scatter. Our citizenship is in heaven, yet our kingdom lives begin with conversion and membership in a church.

THE NARROW & BROAD MISSION

All of this gives shape to the much-debated mission of the church. Tim Chester is exactly right when he argues that the church's mission is both *centripetal* and *centrifugal*. Typically, people view ancient Israel's mission as centripetal, drawing towards a centre – "Come and see us!" (see Deut 4:4-8). The New Testament church, on the other hand, is said to possess a centrifugal, outward mission – "Go into all nations" (Matt 28:19). But that's not quite right. What's really changed, says Chester, is the centre. Churches and church planters should go, but when they go, they establish what I'm calling embassies of the eschaton, doorways into another dimension, or time machines for the nations to come and see what Christ's future rule will look like.

www.thegospelcoalition.org/article/mission-of-god-see-church

For a chapter-length discussion of the church's narrow and broad mission see my contribution to *Four Views on The Church's Mission*, edited by Jason S. Sexton (Downers Grove, IL: Zondervan, 2017), 17-45.

Furthermore, the centrifugal and centripetal elements of a church's mission correspond, vaguely, with the narrow and broad aspects of its mission. The distinction here requires us to think of a church in two different ways or in two different moments of its life. Corresponding to the centrifugal motion, the church *as an organised collective or corporate actor* (the church jointly) possesses a narrow mission: make disciples and citizens of Christ's kingdom. Through the pulpit and membership decisions, a church employs priest-like words of formal separation, identification, and instruction: "This is the gospel," "This is not the gospel," "She is a believer," "He is not a believer," "This is the way of obedience," "This is not." The ordinances speak and seal these decisions, binding and loosing on earth what's bound and loosed in heaven. This narrow mission should condition the bulk of what a church does together, including what it does in its services or through its budget. It should also constrain a pastor's job description.

Corresponding to the centripetal motion, the church *as its individual members* (the church severally) possesses a broad mission: live as disciples and citizens in all the ways that Jesus has commanded. This broad mission should characterise the lives of the saints all week, whether gathered or scattered. It calls us to live and rule as sons of the King, representing the heavenly Father in all our words and deeds. If the decisions and judgments of the church-as-a-corporate-actor are conscience-binding, the church-as-its-members abide in the domain of Christian liberty as they pursue their broad mission. One saint might decide to represent Christ's righteousness *this* way; another saint might decide to work for God's justice *that* way. One gets married, one remains single (see 1 Cor 7). One is convinced that abstaining from meat is holy, another is not (see Rom 14). Yet the purpose of all is to represent the image of Christ and the rule of the Father.

The relationship between the narrow and the broad look like this:

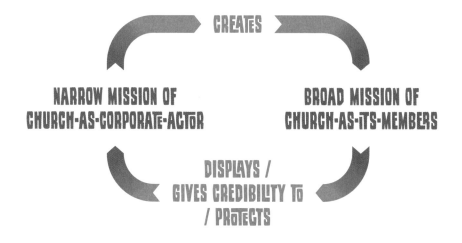

CREATES

NARROW MISSION OF CHURCH-AS-CORPORATE-ACTOR

BROAD MISSION OF CHURCH-AS-ITS-MEMBERS

DISPLAYS / GIVES CREDIBILITY TO / PROTECTS

The narrow mission creates the broad, while the broad displays, gives credibility to, and protects the narrow. The narrow mission, in a word, is the work of an embassy. The broad mission, in a word, is the work of an ambassador.

How can church leaders and members help our congregations offer an attractive and honest apologetic for the gospel? How do we grow in looking like we're genuinely from the future? Here are six recommendations:

BEGIN WITH WORD MINISTRY

First, the gathered church should give itself over to preaching, singing, praying, and reading God's word. The word alone gives life, replaces hearts, gives sight, grants faith. Your charisma as a preacher does not, my cleverness as a teacher does not. The word makes the church alive, holy, and distinct. It divides between the righteous and the unrighteous, and it points to the unrighteousness inside of us. A church that waters down God's word will have a watered-down discipleship. A church that abandons God's word will abandon its discipleship. A church that preaches meaty expositional sermons through every genre and book of the Bible is a church whose members will grow in grace, wisdom, and understanding.

ALWAYS DO GOSPEL MINISTRY

Second, our expositions of Scripture, our counselling, and our fellowship should centre on the gospel. Too easily do ministers take the gospel for granted. Too easily do the saints succumb to moralism. Learning to interpret every text canonically is a crucial part of this, but so is remembering that most sermons, counselling sessions, and words of correction to a fellow member should include not just words about what the saints must do, but what Christ has done. Justification by faith alone, with its talk of a vicarious righteousness, is the counter-intuitive and unworldly wisdom that makes no sense to our self-righteously political and self-sufficiently therapeutic age. Want to write a best-selling book? Write a motivational book, a how-to book, a prosperity gospel book, or a spirituality and wellness book. You'll sell millions because people love knowing what they must do. Every morning I wake up as a self-justifier and wannabe self-ruler. Every day and in every sermon, therefore, I need reminding that God blesses the poor in spirit and the mourning, because that is not my fallen heart's natural posture. All of a church's teaching and counselling and praying and singing, publicly and privately, should work through the lens of the gospel.

PRACTICE MEMBERSHIP AND DISCIPLINE

Third, churches should practice membership and discipline. If the churches look just like the world, why would they heed our message? The failure to practice meaningful membership and discipline, in other words, will undermine a church's preaching. Therefore, churches should receive as full-communing members only those who know the gospel and have committed themselves to living by it. Paul therefore exhorts the Corinthians to put out of their fellowship a man who is sleeping with his mother in law. Later, he tells them to "come out and be separate" from false teaching and living more broadly. Lightness and darkness, Christ and Belial, have nothing in common, he says. He exhorts the Galatian churches (not the leaders, but the churches) to put out anyone who preaches a false gospel, even if that preacher plays the apostle or angel-in-heaven card, never mind the bishop or pastor card. John tells his readers to test the spirits by making sure the spirits affirm that Jesus came in the flesh. Jesus himself tells the church to put out of its fellowship anyone who will not repent in a dispute with a brother or sister.

Different churches will have different ways of practicing membership and discipline. Generally, I would encourage churches to consider what my church does: hold membership classes so that people know what they are committing to. Require membership interviews where pastors or elders ask prospective members about their spiritual journey and for an explanation of the gospel. Share the name and testimony of the prospective member first with the elders and then with the entire congregation, asking the church to affirm each individual. This whole church must know for whom they are responsible – who the different parts are (see 1 Cor 12). Preach corporate applications every week, explaining what different passages mean for the church's life together. Remind the congregation regularly of their need to build relationships where they can have meaningful conversations. Encourage them to practice church discipline privately with loving words of correction and encouragement. Teach and eventually practice church discipline publicly, warning and then putting out of membership anyone who proves unrepentant for serious and outward (everyone agrees on the facts) sin. Few things destroy a church's apologetic witness more quickly than a lack of discipline. Contrary to timid Christian intuitions, church membership and discipline are crucial to a church's evangelism. Speaking of which...

CULTIVATE A CULTURE OF EVANGELISM

Being a time machine from the future presumes we tell people we're from the future, or rather, that Christ's kingdom is coming and they, too, must repent and believe. Salvation does not come through one's parents or membership in the Church of England. There is no such thing as a Christian country or family. It does not come to those who do good and mean well.

God's final judgment is irrevocable, awful, and certain. His love is expansive, exquisite, and eternal. Yet people must repent and believe. They must be *converted*, as intolerant as such a word sounds today. People must cross over from death to life by calling upon the name of the Lord, because everyone who calls upon the name of the Lord will be saved.

Churches, therefore, should encourage and equip their members to share the gospel. Use sermons, Sunday Schools, and small groups to train. Evangelism programmes are okay. Tools and training for evangelism are better. A culture of evangelism, where members treat sharing the gospel as an ordinary part of the Christian life, is best. Pastors and elders can cultivate a culture of evangelism by doing it themselves. When pastors don't evangelise, members don't either.

Evangelism is not sharing a testimony. It's not promising people purpose or blessing or riches if they would only give to Jesus. It's not doing apologetics or talking about Christianity in clever philosophical terms. Evangelism begins by announcing a judge's verdict: "You're guilty and under condemnation." It continues with the announcement of a king's promise: "The King has given his own Son to pay the penalty and offer a way of pardon." And it concludes with a call: "You must repent and believe."

Churches that don't evangelise undermine their own message. I'm unconvinced of your message if you won't even share it. They will eventually shrivel and die.

CULTIVATE A CULTURE OF DISCIPLING AND HOSPITALITY

Living things grow. Therefore, we should expect for Christians to grow. Moreover, true followers of Jesus will help others to follow Jesus. It makes no sense to say you're following Jesus if you're not devoted to helping others follow Jesus. Again, a church's leaders must set the example of giving their days and evenings and meals and trips to the grocery store and time in the yard to helping others follow Jesus. "Can you help me with the overgrown bamboo in my back yard?" "Can I buy you lunch?" "Can I come over and help you with your laundry?" Church leaders and members should constantly be on the search for opportunities to interact with one another so that they might grow in the faith together. After all, families live together, and bodies depend on each part.

One practical tool my own church uses for this is a church membership directory. We work hard at keeping it updated and accurate, so that leaders and members know who "we" are. Many of us place it in our Bibles and pray through a column or page every day during our quiet times. Those prayers often turn into emails or texts: "Prayed for you this morning. How are you doing?" And those emails or texts turn into coffees or meals: "Doing just so-so. Wanna hang out?"

A church's hospitality should extend beyond its own members and pour out to neighbours, colleagues, and beyond. Non-Christians in my own city seldom invite others into their home for a meal. Here is an easy way for Christians to stand out as distinct. Friendships with unbelievers should be ordinary – in the workplace, in the neighbourhood, on the sidelines of the children's football games. Of course, this takes time. One of the greatest hindrances to friendship, hospitality, and evangelism just might be the busyness of our schedules. Are you willing to slow down and prioritise such friendships?

ENSURE THE ELDERS MODEL EVANGELISM AND DISCIPLING

I've seen it again and again: where the elders of a church consistently evangelise and disciple, you will find an evangelistic and discipling church. Where they don't, you won't.

This makes sense when you think about what God has created an elder to be. He is not a different kind of Christian, like a blue-blooded member of the aristocracy or a medieval priest. Nor is he a picture of "advanced Christianity." Rather, an elder should live as an example of "basic Christianity." His job is to disciple people to be like him – "Follow me as I follow Christ." This is why Paul's character qualifications for elders are so ordinary – they should characterise *every* Christian with the exception of "not a recent convert" and "able to teach."

What your church needs, in other words, is a plurality of men who faithfully define with their lives what ordinary Christianity looks like. When evangelism and discipling are ordinary for them, they will become ordinary for the church.

CONCLUSION

It's not cultural nostalgia that churches today need, or strategies for the culture war, or a vision for a nation. Yet nor should churches seclude themselves and forsake their neighbours. Instead, churches must engage the world with something otherworldly. They must respond to cultural chaos with a new culture; to a divided nation as a new nation; to broken families as God's family. They are to be what they are – time machines from the future.

Amidst social change, therefore, our focus must fall first upon our churches (see 1 Pet 4:17). We shouldn't talk about sex trafficking if we are viewing pornography. Or racial reconciliation if our churches are divided. Or welfare politics if we're not generous. We are the ones whose hearts of stone have been made flesh through the gospel.

The more Western culture opposes God and his people, therefore, the more the gospel distinctiveness of our churches should shine. Opposition sets a backdrop for the display of the glory of God in our lives.

Psalm 67:1-2 | *May God be gracious to us and bless us and make his face shine on us, so that your ways may be known on earth, your salvation among all nations.*

How do we respond to ominous cultural changes? By being the church, whether together or apart, that the nations might know the way of God.

For further reading see my *Church Membership: How the World Knows Who Represents Jesus* (Crossway, 2012), *Church Discipline: How the Church Protects the Name of Jesus* (Crossway, 2012), and *How the Nations Rage: Rethinking Faith and Politics for a Divided Age* (Thomas Nelson, 2018). Many of these ideas have been developed at length and in academic terms in *Political Church: the Local Assembly as Embassy of Christ's Rule* (IVP Academic, 2016).

See also Mark Dever, *Discipling: How to Help Others Follow Jesus* (Crossway, 2017) and Mack Stiles, *Evangelism: How the Whole Church Speaks of Jesus* (Crossway, 2014).

Questions for further thought and discussion

1. How is the gospel "church-shaped"?

2. What does justification by faith have to do with the life of the church?

3. If the church's mission has both a centripetal and a centrifugal force, how is/could that be reflected in the life of your church?

4. In the face of objections to the biblical teaching about sexuality, gender and injustice, Jonathan argues that we need to create and sustain:

   ⇒ *flourishing adolescents, singles, and marriages, where those who stumble into this or that temptation find themselves meaningfully embraced by a new-creation family.*

   ⇒ *a culture of happy, strong, and engaged women.*

   ⇒ *a culture of discipling and good deeds, where congregations present a picture of true justice and righteousness, both within themselves and spilling outward.*

   What concrete steps could your church take towards those?

GETTING BEHIND THE WALL

PREACHING AND APOLOGETICS

In his commentary on Romans, John Calvin underlines the connection between the calling of God, the preaching of the word of God, and saving faith:

> *There can be no true invoking of God's name unless such invocation has been preceded by a correct knowledge of Him. Moreover, faith arises from the Word of God. But wherever the Word of God is preached, it is only by the special providence and appointment of God. Faith, therefore, exists where God is invoked; where there is faith, it has been preceded by the seed of the Word; and where there is preaching there is the calling of God.*

Consequently, argues Calvin,

> *There is a clear and undoubted sign of the divine goodness where His calling is thus effective and productive of fruit. It will finally be established from this that the Gentiles... are not to be excluded from the kingdom of God. For as the preaching of the Gospel is the cause of faith among them, so the mission of God, by which it pleased Him to provide for their salvation in this manner, is the cause of preaching.*

Calvin's New Testament Commentaries – The Epistles of Paul to the Romans and Thessalonians (eds. David W. Torrance and Thomas F. Torrance; trans. R Mackenzie; Grand Rapids: Eerdmans, 1960), 230. The passage on which Calvin is commenting is Romans 10:13.

GAVIN MCGRATH is Associate Rector at St Nicholas Church, Sevenoaks. He has ministered in Anglican churches in the USA and Durham, Sheffield, and London, as well as teaching at English L'Abri and serving as Vice-Principal of Trinity School for Ministry (Pittsburgh, PA USA).

Here's the point: The word of God is the way God calls people to saving faith in the Lord Jesus and, so, the word of God preached to the world is **central to the mission of God in the world.**

This isn't to minimise the importance of good works, social justice advocacy, or works of mercy. When I use the word 'central' I mean what is central or of primary importance. Central doesn't mean only.

In light of those connections, we are going to explore a few key questions:

- *What does it mean to preach the word of God?*

- *What does the word of God do?*

- *And how does it do it?*

Looking at these will move us towards a discussion of what I call *apologetic preaching*. So, to begin with: what does it mean to preach the word of God?

PREACHING THE WORD OF GOD MEANS PROCLAIMING GOD'S PROMISES

The church of God grows and advances by the word of God even in the midst of attack and persecution. Luke makes this point throughout Acts (see, for example, Acts 6:7; 12:24 and 19:20).

This word is God's word about his King, the Lord Jesus Christ. That too is clear from Acts. Apostolic preaching focuses on him as God's Christ, the risen Lord and coming Judge. And the Holy Spirit applies *this* preaching to the hearts and minds of those called to faith. By this we (as hearers or readers of Acts) see how the crucified, risen, and ascended Jesus really is the Saviour of the world. In a similar way, when Paul refers to the gospel he places primary emphasis on the gospel as a statement about Jesus Christ – risen Lord, coming Judge, and present Saviour. Only then does he speak about the benefits of the gospel to those who repent and believe in Jesus (see Romans 1:1-6). The gospel then, is all about the Lord Jesus Christ – who he is, what he has done, and what he will do. It is vital to get this right!

Of course, apostolic preaching did not occur in a vacuum: there were accompanying signs, healings, miracles and confirming incidents. Moreover, the apostolic lifestyle – transparent love, care, godly character, and constant prayer – adorned the apostolic ministries. Still, central (again, appreciate what central means) to apostolic ministry is the preaching of God's word. And God's word is supremely about God's anointed Son, the Lord Jesus Christ.

As a consequence, the central component of the apostolic ministry was **preaching**; preaching as proclamation and teaching (see Acts 20:17-38; 1 Cor 1:17; Phil 1:18; 1 Tim 3:2; 4:6-16; 6:2; 20; 2 Tim 2:1-2,14-16, 22-26; 3:10-17; and 4:1-8).

So far nothing I've said is new to most readers – it is probably a shared conviction. So, let me sharpen my focus. To do this, I want to emphasise that the word of God about the Lord Jesus Christ is not only news for the world it is also God's *promise* to the world. God makes particular promises and keeps these promises. We need to know the promise that Jesus Christ is Saviour and Lord. **This is the nature of God's word.**

I remain deeply indebted to the fine explanation of promise made by Peter Jensen, *The Revelation of God* (Downers Grove: IVP, 2002), 60, 70-83.

To think of the gospel as *promise* opens the door to a new understanding of preaching. It isn't simply talking about news – even good news – it is heralding a promise from the promise-making and promise-keeping triune God. The promise is good because the one promising it is good. The promise depends upon the intention of the promise maker and the ability of the promise maker to fulfil the promise. Intentionality, capability, and reliability – these all relate to God's 'side' of the promise.

But there is an additional feature here: suitability. God's promise to men and women in the gospel of the Lord Jesus Christ is suitable (fitting, relevant, or appropriate) to who we are as men and women in whatever social context, historical context, or situational context.

In his word God promises to address the *decreation* caused by human rebellion and sin and bring in *recreation*. His word is a promise to judge and punish human rebellion against him. His word is a promise to judge human wickedness towards other humans, human idolatries, and human exploitation of creation. His word is a promise that God keeps his word – his word of judgment but also his word of salvation through his Son, the Lord Jesus Christ. His word is a real promise to those who *now* trust Christ's righteousness and his penal substitutionary death on the cross (he took my place instead of me bearing the penalty I deserve). He promises that those who *now* trust in his Son are freely pardoned and loved. He promises them that they are progressively changed *now* for the coming great day when Christ will fully establish his Kingdom. To sum up then, the Bible is best seen as a promissory word. That raises our question: how does the word of God persuade us to see the world God's way and embrace his promises?

The terms *decreation* and *recreation* come from Steve Jeffrey, Mike Ovey, and Andrew Sach, *Pierced for Our Transgressions – Rediscovering the Glory of Penal Substitution* (Nottingham: IVP, 2007), 110-12. By *decreation* they mean the way that the fall "reverses and undoes the ordered network of relationships God created;" by *recreation*, they highlight the way that salvation involves a new work of God to restore and fulfil creation's purposes.

WHAT DOES THE WORD OF GOD DO, AND HOW DOES IT DO IT?

So far, I have been saying the one true God is the speaking, promise-extending God. Now we need to see that the triune God extends his promises to people today in his written word, the Bible. This is a vast topic requiring careful, humble, and faithful study beyond the space allotted to me here. But with the help of some beneficial resources we can highlight the following aspects of God's word as promise-containing texts.

First, we tend to forget that God speaks in human texts that function as texts – in other words, they convey meaning in the same ways that people do when they talk or communicate with one another. Hardly any conversation is a simple information transfer, or

Two more stretching and technical works are: Kevin J. Vanhoozer, *Is There a Meaning in This Text? The Bible, the Reader, and the Morality of Literary Knowledge* (Grand Rapids: Zondervan, 1998); and Nicholas Wolterstorff, *Divine Discourse: Philosophical Reflections on the Claim that God Speaks* (Cambridge: Cambridge University Press, 1995). The most lucid and accessible distillation of these works and others is by Timothy Ward, *Words of Life: Scripture as the Living and Active Word of God* (Nottingham: IVP, 2009).

reducible to a few key propositions, and yet we so often approach the Bible as if it is. This is profoundly important, as I hope to show later in this article.

Second, the purpose of biblical texts is to convey revelation, but revelation specifically focused on promise – the gospel. Yet the *how* – the genre – of the actual text of Scripture also matters. Consequently, we pay close attention to the content of revelation and to the functional ways the differing genres communicate this revelation. This means, for example, we see how an epistle functions grammatically, linguistically, and rhetorically. In another example, say, poetry, we will look not only for the theological content but also at the ways this content comes to us. In the particular case of poetry (and we could probably say the same thing about narrative material) we will try to avoid reducing everything to simple declarative sentences because this is precisely what poetry does not do. In other words, both the content of the genre and the genre style tell us what to communicate and how to communicate.

Third, because of this last point, preaching that takes the biblical texts seriously will want to draw out both meaning and implications of the biblical texts. But we will do this sensitive to literary functions. This is because the very text itself *functions* in certain ways. I am referring not only to genre characteristics but even more so to the ways texts function as speech-acts. This is a complicated area, but think of it this way:

Say I want to pass on to a friend my mobile telephone number. I do so in a particular way or with a particular functional style: straightforward informing "My number is…". My aim is to *inform*. But suppose I want to give my mobile number to my friend because I want to *assure* my friend I will collect him at the railway station at a specific time. I give this assurance in a particular way, with a specific action involved – in this case a promise or assurance. This communication is stylistically and functionally different than when I am driving my friend back to my home and we chat about our work, our family, and, most certainly, when my friend tells me another one of his poor jokes! His aim is to *amuse*. You and I normally understand communication's speech-act intention and function because we are sensitive (knowingly or unknowingly) to how communication works.

Where am I going here? My point is this: biblical texts are not simply 'acting' to inform or even 'to teach'. They certainly do both but not as we often assume. Because biblical texts act as extending word(s) of promise they often communicate or 'act' in ways addressing our minds but via our affections, imagination, and unconscious desires. Consider, for example, how biblical texts in which God extends his promises to us, employ 'surprise.'

Surprises – what we the readers do not expect or anticipate – are frequently generated by Scripture and they are important *means* of God conveying both his promise and its implications.

An example is in order. Say we are preaching on the story of David and Goliath (1 Samuel 17). This is narrative material. It is a cracking story! Accordingly, our treatment of this text is sensitive to narrative in the Bible.

Narrative is truth set in a structure of characters who run into a problem, reaching a crisis, finding a resolution, and concluding with a summation. Biblical narratives usually tell us the primary character of the story is not us, the reader. In the story of David and Goliath it is ultimately about God and God's anointed king (see Hannah's song in 2:1-10, and especially the last verse). We are not to ask, "How do I relate to David?" Rather, because of the overall structure of 1 and 2 Samuel, we are compelled to ask, "What is this story telling us about who God is and what God promises?"

And then come the surprises within the actual text. What is the surprise (appreciating there are probably lots of surprises!)? Is it not the surprise that Goliath – Israel's enemy – is defeated by a weak and vulnerable little boy? It is not what we would expect. Moreover, see how the surprise launches us on a trajectory (itself what we would not expect). It is not that Goliath is simply Israel's enemy; Goliath stands in opposition to the God of Israel himself. In this respect, God's enemy is defeated in the weakness and vulnerability of a little boy: not *despite* weakness and vulnerability, but *through* weakness and vulnerability.

And within the overall storyline of 1 and 2 Samuel we learn God's anointed king will truly be great but not by the standards or means of greatness we recognise. Supremely, God's anointed king – the Lord Jesus Christ – is the one to whom the story of David and Goliath points (see Luke 24:25-27 and 44-49).

So, here we see how the gospel – *the* central promise God proclaims to humanity – confounds human expectations and assumptions. In the first instance, we see we are *not* David. Truth is, we more closely relate to the cowering army of Israel who are only 'saved' by the intervention of God's man – not Saul but David. And the promise is that God saves his people who trust in the Saviour God sends: the Lord Jesus Christ, the heir of David.

Surprises like this in the story of David and Goliath catch us unaware. The surprise subverts our preconceptions in a number of ways. We might come to the story of David and Goliath assuming that the story is urging us to be daring and brave in faith like David; but this, actually, only serves to strengthen the idol of our self-reliance and threatens to reduce the story to a moralistic cliché. The surprise of the little boy's weakness can subvert not only our preconceived notions of power and greatness; it can also subvert our notion of what we understand our personal strengths and greatness to be. And this kind of surprise is conveyed within the language, syntax and literary function of texts. Accordingly, our preaching should aim to communicate the gospel by employing the communication style of the biblical texts.

APOLOGETIC PREACHING

At least in my mind, apologetic preaching does not involve a series entitled 'Has science disproved the Bible?' or 'Is Christian faith intolerant?' or 'What human sexuality is really all about'. These kinds of topical preaching series may (or may not) have their place, but they are not what I mean by apologetic preaching.

To begin with, apologetic preaching is preaching based on what we have considered so far in this article:

> *We aim to let the Scriptures sit in the 'driver's seat'.*

> *More specifically, we take seriously what the texts are trying to **do** – the speech-act intentionality and functionality of the biblical texts.*

> *We focus on the way in which God's word holds out the promises of God.*

To this we can now add some other basic premises which will be familiar if you have read the earlier articles in this issue of *Primer*, and then sketch out more clearly what apologetic preaching might look like.

1. HUMAN NATURE

Humanity is made in the image of God but is radically fallen. Every aspect of our being is now corrupt and engaged in rebellion against God. We are spiritually dead towards God. At the same time, we are still human. We have not lost this distinct identity. In theological shorthand we can say that the catastrophe described in Genesis 3 (in which we all share and experience) has not totally ruptured the reality described in Genesis 1 and 2. Consequently, God addresses fallen humanity which is still human. Therefore, like preaching in general, apologetic preaching is God addressing fallen humanity, but humanity nonetheless.

In other words, there is a complementary reality. As humans we are still image-bearers, living in a God-created and sustained universe. Even though we are fallen and totally corrupted by corporate and personal sin and guilt towards God, there is an irrepressible God-consciousness (see Rom 1:19-20). This is not a human virtue independent from God; it is because God creates us and we are living in his universe that we still have this awareness. It is what Calvin called the *"seed of religion."*

John Calvin, *Institutes of the Christian Religion* (Library of Christian Classics; ed. John T. McNeill; trans. Ford Lewis Battles; Philadelphia: Westminster, 1960), I.iv.1.

There is no natural theology: on our own and by nature we pervert the witness within creation and within ourselves: we fall into superstition, idolatry, and other expressions of spiritual ignorance; in fact, we even deny we are God's creatures made in his image. At the same time there is an irrepressible 'echo' within creation and even within ourselves confirming we are God's creatures living in God's creation. This is the complementary reality: God's word does not come to us describing one reality while we live in an entirely different reality. Apologetic preaching, therefore, is not essentially alien or foreign to us (although, it seems this way to us at first). Of course, on our own we hate divine revelation and want nothing of it; such is the serious tragedy of our sinfulness.

2. THE SIGNIFICANCE OF OUR CULTURAL CONTEXT

At one level, context is irrelevant. There is "nothing new under the sun" when it comes to the human problem. In this sense the gospel diagnoses and then addresses men and women in every age, culture, and social setting. No one age or social context is harder or easier to reach with the gospel. We err if we suggest that our age and context necessitates a reconfiguration of the gospel on the assumption that some aspects of biblical revelation don't fit within our context anymore.

On another level, though, context is highly relevant. We are all set within a particular time/space/place/social context. We are not disembodied or timeless beings. We are humans set within God's created world in our specific place and in our specific time and commissioned to proclaim the gospel in that specific place and time.

This is why, for example, **Charles Taylor's work is invaluable.** His writing is tough going and not immediately accessible; but, with persistence, Taylor's insights are important, even if we might disagree at some points. Taylor helps us understand the difficulty contemporary westerners have holding to traditional religious beliefs. Of course, it is a matter of rebellion and sin (both individual and collective). But the manifestation of this sin and rebellion have particular causes and dynamics – all of which we should be aware. The dominance of the autonomous self explains why and how contemporary people prefer 'spirituality' over and against, say, traditional Christian belief and practice. There are many causes and reinforcements of our contemporary conclusion about the "implausibility" of the gospel.

Two important works by Taylor are, *The Sources of the Self: The Making of the Modern Identity* (Cambridge, Mass.: Harvard University Press, 1992) and *A Secular Age* (Cambridge, Mass.: Harvard University Press, 2007). As mentioned, these are daunting works! Some helpful summaries of and engagements with Taylor are: James K. A. Smith, *How (Not) to be Secular: Reading Charles Taylor* (Grand Rapids: Eerdmans, 2014) and Collin Hansen (ed.), *Our Secular Age: Ten Years of Reading and Applying Charles Taylor* (Deerfield: The Gospel Coalition, 2017).

3. THE SIGNIFICANCE OF PRESUPPOSITIONS

Biblical preaching always occurs within the complementary reality just mentioned: human beings are made in the image of God and yet are now broken images. That is always true, and will find expression in countless different ways in each generation and culture, just as it has in our own secular age. Consequently, in apologetic preaching, it is important to make what we can call *complementary moves*. In this model we move over to the ground of the unbeliever (and the unbelief which even believers battle) and show that his or her worldview, mental map, and presuppositions do not

Cornelius Van Til, *Christian Apologetics* (ed. William Edgar; Philipsburg: P&R 2003), 39.

work and are inconsistent. We seek to persuade people that non-Christian worldviews provide no real and authentic basis for meaning and value. Van Til called this *predication*: namely, without the existence of the God of Christianity (the Father, the Son and the Holy Spirit) nothing can rightly and truly be said to exist or make sense. From this comes what Van Til calls 'the removal of the iron mask' or what Schaeffer describes as 'taking the roof off' contemporary men and women's worldviews.

With these three factors in view, we can now develop this idea of apologetic preaching.

APOLOGETIC PREACHING IN PRACTICE

Preaching that is apologetic aims to get 'behind the wall' of contemporary hearers. This is true to the texts of the Bible themselves. Often, as I mentioned earlier, they employ subversive surprises. This is why I stressed the crucial importance of preachers taking seriously both the content of the Bible and the manner in which the Bible communicates this content. Apologetic preaching is best done as the preacher asks questions of the text, hears what the text is saying and promising, and then asks questions about both the text and contemporary men and women. So, in this respect, apologetic preaching is exegetical and expositional. It has to be if it seeks to understand, teach, proclaim, and apply the Bible. But it involves more than we sometimes realise: careful listening for the text's worldview presuppositions and implications, and then tuning into the ways the text does its apologetic probing, examining, questioning, wooing, and persuading.

I hasten to add here that that which restricts is far, far more than intellectual objection! The matters of the heart and will are, I increasingly suspect, weightier than many of us understand. See the stimulating work by James K. A. Smith, *You Are What You Love* (Grand Rapids: Brazos, 2016). See also the important non-Christian works: Jonathan Haidt, *The Righteous Mind: Why Good People are Divided by Politics and Religion* (London: Penguin, 2012) and Margaret Heffernan, *Wilful Blindness: Why we Ignore the Obvious at our Peril* (London: Simon & Shuster, 2011).

As the preacher does so, they are better able to anticipate the 'stuff' restricting contemporary people from responding to God's word. Here is what I mean by the 'stuff': sitting behind/beside the person in the pew are cultural voices and persuaders. By persuaders we can think of the voices and influences in our entertainment, education, literature, mass marketing, parental and familial values, and so on. Consequently, there is nothing remotely like a neutral or unbiased position we can take as we listen to God's word. Experientially and culturally our own heart and mind inclination is towards disbelief, idolatry, and rebellion. Moreover, as cultural fragmentation increases, and secularisation continues, the plausibility of Christianity will increasingly appear questionable – even among Christians!

In practice, therefore, a simple proclamation of God's word has limited impact. This is what we might call 'thin' apologetics – true, accurate and orthodox theology taught, proclaimed and delivered. What is missing is both an appreciation of how biblical texts convey theological truth and how apologetics help us get behind the wall of 'stuff.'

But 'thick' apologetics does this. It questions all of the promises and interpretations of contemporary ideas, theories, values and conceptions offered by the cultural voices and persuaders. It is not simply a proclamation of theological truths; it is a presentation of the Bible's texts so that people can hear God speak to them, call them, challenge them, and promise them the gospel. God's own speaking deconstructs their flawed worldview and erroneous presuppositions and, thereby, shows them the incompleteness of their living.

An example is called for here and I want to select one many would not immediately consider having any apologetic implications – again, this is because too often we hear 'apologetic' and assume it has to deal with 'science versus faith' or 'the reliability of the Bible' or 'other religions'. But, frankly, this is to seriously reduce apologetics to 'hot topic questions' – questions, I find, most people (other than Christians) are not asking.

So, suppose we are preaching on the Parable of the Sower in Mark 4:1-20. To start, we appreciate this is within a Gospel, a type or genre which has its own characteristics. Second, we work hard at understanding where Mark places this parable within the overall structure of his Gospel. We see it is before the crucial narrative shift of chapter 8:31, where Jesus begins openly to teach his disciples of his impending sufferings and their necessity. So, the big question so far in Mark's Gospel is, "Who is this Jesus?" Third, therefore, our ear is attuned to what Mark is telling us about Jesus and his ministry, not ours.

He is not simply calling for us to tell stories or parables or to use imagination in our preaching. Rather, Jesus provides the interpretative key to this parable in 4:10-20. We see that preceding this parable is the incredulity and disbelief of the crowd (3:20-21), the blasphemy of the scribes (3:22-30) and the faithlessness of Jesus' own immediate family (3:31-35). Immediately following the parable is a set of images that assure Jesus' followers that the gospel and kingdom will advance and grow, despite opposition. So, then, the parable chiefly (not exclusively) is telling us something about Jesus' ministry, opposition to Jesus' ministry, and, yet, the eventual triumph of Jesus' ministry.

Now, where is the surprise in this parable? Arguably, there are many. One of the surprises is that Jesus – God's Son and King – is all too easily rejected. Doesn't it seem that this rejection is because there is something wrong with him or his message? Yet surprisingly, the problem is not with Jesus but with those who hear him. It is not the gospel that is the problem but the ways we hear the gospel. And in the parable Jesus presents different ways people hear. In fact, Jesus calls his listeners to listen well (4:9). But the biggest surprise that ought quietly and subtly to work on us is the promise Jesus makes that, despite all signs to the contrary, the gospel of the kingdom will produce a huge harvest (4:8,20). Surely, this is Jesus' ultimate point and why Mark recounts it. We know all too well that there is opposition and resistance. We do not need yet another parable to point this out to us. What we do need to hear and know is the promise that the gospel will advance and that those who do respond with faith and repentance are not doing so in vain – they will be fruitful and their lives will count for something real, both here and now, and in the future kingdom.

The apologetic implications, therefore, emerge and with them we start to get 'behind the wall' of contemporary hearers. What is the fundamental claim of secularism or atheism? It is that Christianity is hopelessly irrelevant and useless. In secular Europe the media constantly tell us that Christianity is declining and church attendance demonstrates this. 'Behind the wall' of many (and this will include those who are Christian) is the nagging suspicion Christianity may well be irrelevant and diminishing. So, why not quietly slip away from gospel things and gospel living?

But Mark's text here is the extension both of a warning but more importantly of a gracious promise and assurance. It is God's promise that the voices of cultural scepticism, cynicism, and emptiness are wrong. God promises the allure of materialism and consumerism are illusions in light of the sure promise of the gospel. Surely, we need to hear this and the way it works on some of the cultural presuppositions of our day. Surely, the Parable of the Sower is more than a model of evangelistic strategy or a call for all preachers to tell more stories using agricultural images! It is, thankfully, God's promise in a text that functionally promises. A story that subverts the narratives of our culture.

CONCLUSION: THE BRINGING OF GLAD TIDINGS OF DELIVERANCE

As Bill Edgar puts it,

*William Edgar,
Reasons of the
Heart: recovering
Christian persuasion
(Grand Rapids, IL:
Baker, 1996), 26.*

...the reason today or any day represents a special opportunity – the reason that apologetics is relevant – is not primarily because we have a good understanding of the cultural context. Rather it is because of the message, the good news of the gospel.

It is precisely because of the gospel itself that we are compelled to speak to contemporary men and women. Our apologetics, then, is to be gospel-shaped, gospel-driven, and gospel-aimed. We speak what the gospel speaks. We address what the gospel addresses. We confront what the gospel confronts. And we do all of this in the way and the manner of the word of God.

All of this means apologetic preaching seems to resonate with Scripture's approach and with the method of Scripture as a collected body of different genres – poetry, epistle, gospel and, overwhelmingly, narrative. This in turn gives rise to a preaching of the Bible that functions apologetically.

Questions for further thought and discussion

1. Why is it helpful to think of the Bible as a book trying to persuade us to believe God's promises?

2. How might that thought affect the way we prepare sermons or pray before God's word is read?

3. According to Gavin, 'apologetic preaching' has nothing to do with topical talks. So what, in a nutshell, is it?

4. Can you think of any other examples of texts that provide subversive surprises?

ANSWERS ON THE GROUND

Central to *Primer* is a desire to help you see the difference good theology makes to the life of a local church. So, in keeping with this issue's topic, we interviewed leaders from three churches who are thoughtfully and creatively wrestling with the apologetic challenges of their diverse communities.

STEPHEN KNEALE is Pastor at Oldham Bethel Church, Greater Manchester. He is the author of *Being a Christian: The Basics of Christian Living* and regularly writes on theological, political and social issues on his blog at *StephenKneale.com*.

 @steve_kneale

1. How would you describe the community you are seeking to reach?

At Oldham Bethel Church, we have three main constituencies we are seeking to reach. First, our immediate area is replete with South Asian Muslims, primarily from Pakistan and Bangladesh. Within this group there are first generation immigrants, as well as second and third generation British Muslims. Some are devout Sunni Muslim – with many of the local mosques being funded with Saudi money and thus come with a large side-order of **Wahhabi Salafism** – while others are nominally Muslim at best.

Second, we have an ongoing ministry to a good number of

Salafi Wahhabism is an ultra-conservative, fundamentalist brand of Islamic thought emanating from Saudi Arabia. It is the version of Islam that many cite as the foundation of ISIL and Al-Qaeda, providing the religious underpinning for much Islamist terrorism.

Iranian asylum seekers. Most of these are culturally Zoroastrian but raised Shia Muslim. Many of those with us have experienced severe torture at the hands of their Islamic theocratic government. By the time they reach the UK, having experienced the sharp end of Islam – and being culturally Zoroastrian and thus viewing the Islamic faith as an occupying force – many have simply rejected the faith in which they were raised and are looking for something else.

Third, there is a substantial white British working-class community. Much of Oldham remains highly segregated with almost exclusively white estates separated from predominantly Asian areas. Our area of Glodwick has historically been considered a no-go area for white Brits. It was the epicentre of the 2001 race riots in the town. Like most indigenous Brits, most people on the estates know nothing of the gospel and are biblically illiterate. However, Atheism does not reign. Most believe in some sort of god but tend to live as though he has no real interest in their lives and they pay him little attention.

2. What are the major apologetic challenges or questions you encounter?

As you can imagine, the apologetic issues we encounter differ widely between these groups. Most South Asian Muslims have no problem with some of the harder Christian doctrines that many middle-class communities would like to play down. We have broad agreement that hell exists, God is a judge and Jesus will come again. Most of their issues stem from the doctrine of the Trinity. They particularly cannot accept that God would become man, it is just too dishonouring on their view. As a result, they struggle with penal substitution, but have no basis on which Allah can be just and merciful simultaneously. They also struggle with the resurrection because the Qur'an explicitly rejects the crucifixion, denying that Jesus even died on the cross. It is also common for them to insist that the Bible has been corrupted, though they will typically have no evidence for the claim.

By contrast, Iranian asylum seekers tend to have fewer apologetic issues. Whilst some have converted already in Iran, hence their need to seek asylum in the UK, others arrive at church with a keen interest in the gospel. Many ask, almost as soon as you meet them, how they can become Christians. The issues we face with asylum seekers are less apologetic and more practical. It may seem perverse, but the biggest issue is their eagerness to come to Christ. Given the situation they are in, we are conscious that they have an obvious vested interest in claiming conversion so that we may vouch on their behalf before the Home Office and bolster their claim for asylum. The biggest problem for us is not handling their apologetic questions but whether they are genuine in their desire to come to faith and tackling the root problems hidden in the heart.

The white working class indigenous population have an altogether different set of concerns. In fact, it is hard to pin down any one set of issues. There is certainly much pop secularism, usually gleaned from internet memes, that passes as intelligent argument. Unsurprisingly, in a deprived community like ours, the apologetic arguments tend to centre on God's justice and the problem of suffering. For example, if God cares about us, why are we so poor, why do we face the problems we have, etc? These issues often flow out of the victim-culture that is prevalent in British society. Essentially, I am the victim and I cannot be responsible, therefore the local council, or MPs, or God himself is to blame.

3. As a church, how have you tried to address those issues as you reach out and disciple young believers?

As a church, we are reaching these three groups in different – though sometimes overlapping – fora. With our South Asian friends, we hold regular Muslim-Christian Dialogue evenings. We will choose a topic, both sides will present their respective view and then we have Q&A after each presentation. We share food together after each meeting and rotate the venue between a local mosque and our church building. These meetings have given the opportunity to tackle hard questions head on. We either present on those very issues and then take questions or they often come up in the Q&A giving us the opportunity to address formally in the public meeting and on a more informal basis afterward over food.

We also engage in regular open air evangelism in the town centre. This gives really good interaction with local South Asian Muslims as well as white indigenous Oldhammers. Again, we tackle many of those apologetic issues publicly as we speak. However, we also invite interaction and try to have what amounts to a public conversation with real people on the street who have genuine questions. Further, we are able to speak with people one-to-one – using the open air meeting as a focal point – simply to press into people's views and beliefs. These meetings consist of public speaking, direct engagement with the crowd, one-to-one conversations, and the giving of interviews regarding how church members came to faith.

With many of our Iranian asylum seekers, as they are already coming into the church, we treat them similarly to any other church member. The teaching of the church is done formally through preaching, home group Bible studies and men

and women's Bible studies. There are also the more informal ways in which we disciple people through meetups, lunches, coffee, etc. As our Iranian men and women are committed to coming and learning about the gospel, we simply teach them in the ways we teach anybody else. Our home groups are especially set up for us to take questions and dig into the kind of concerns people may have. At least once per month we run some mission training in our home groups. This may be taking questions people have been asked and struggled to answer or questions they're scared they'll be asked and can't answer. Otherwise, we help each other practically by practising how to give a testimony, discussing when we might share our story and equipping people with the confidence to simply open their Bibles with a friend and ask, 'do you want to study this with me?'

4. What are the most helpful resources you have found?

For the apologetic questions that often come from Muslims, specifically those related to trinity Bruce Ware's *The Man Christ Jesus*, Mike Reeves' *The Good God* and, to a lesser extent, Mike Ovey's *Your Will Be Done* have all been useful in addressing some of those issues.

In respect to getting inside the mindset of Muslim people, I have found little better than *Seeking Allah, Finding Jesus* by Nabeel Quershi.

For ministry to the white urban poor Mez McConnell and Mike McKinley are very helpful in *Church in Hard Places* and Tim Chester offers some helpful insights in *Unreached*.

GRACE FORSYTHE grew up in Tranmere, trained at Oak Hill College, and worked at St George's Church in Dagenham for two years before her current role as Women's Worker at Trinity Church Everton. Her role includes one-to-one work, supporting an addiction recovery group, running a toddler group, helping the church with evangelism and running training sessions for church members on biblical counselling.

1. How would you describe the community you are seeking to reach?

Home to two Premiership football clubs, some of the friendliest people you could meet and a with a rich history of immigration from across the globe, Liverpool is a great city to live in!

Everton overlooks Liverpool city centre, in a ward that's ranked among the most deprived in the UK. Those who work earn around £17,000 a year and you can buy a house for around £80,000. You don't need to look far to find evidence of a creation 'awaiting liberation from its bondage to decay'. Some of the biggest social issues include drug and alcohol addiction, mental health struggles, fallout from family breakdown (child poverty is 48%), domestic violence and gang-related gun crime. Unsurprisingly, many of these issues are interconnected and generational and government cuts mean there are fewer resources available to tackle them.

However, it's not all brokenness and struggle. There are a number of voluntary organisations, social enterprises and community groups, created by people seeking to do something good to alleviate the brokenness. These are all glimpses of common grace in a needy area.

2. What are the major apologetic challenges or questions you encounter?

"I can't believe in a God who ignores suffering."

When you see what life looks like for people here, it's easy to empathise with this response. Many are seemingly powerless to escape the brokenness into which they've been born and so have developed a hardness toward the gospel that says "I've always had to fend for myself, so why bother turning to God now?"

We approach this objection with gentleness and patience, but with confidence that the gospel not only makes sense of the mess of our world, but offers the answer. We often talk about Jesus as 'God in skin', who wasn't indifferent to our pain, but took it on so that we could have the hope of living in a world free from brokenness.

"Christianity is for middle class people, I'm not good enough to go to church and my life's too messy anyway."

It's true that in Everton, many people's lives truly *are* a mess. Sadly there have been times when the church has treated them as projects to be fixed, or even ignored, and rejected them. This has been compounded by an unwillingness to accept them as they are, or conversely, to let them in but keep them at arm's length until they conform to the church's way of doing things. In addition, many churchgoers don't live in Everton itself, but travel in from wealthier areas, which reinforces the view that Christians are aloof from reality.

We want people to see that church is a hospital for sinners, not a museum for saints. We all live locally and by joining community groups, shopping locally and sending our children to local schools we seek to incarnate the inclusivity of the gospel message in the way we live alongside the people we are seeking to reach. In doing this, we're able to build genuine relationships that open up doors for us to tell people what the Bible really says about Jesus – the one who welcomes all who come to him.

"I'm a Christian because I went to a faith school" or "my parents were religious"

A conversation with a man in his 60s went something like this:

Him: *"I'm a Christian."*

Me: *"What church do you go to?"*

Him: *"I went to a Catholic school growing up."*

Liverpool has a high proportion of Church schools and for many people a connection to a church is significant because it's a connection to a parent or grandparent. Whilst this is a trend in decline, it means

we have to work hard to undo the deep-rooted misconceptions about what a Christian is. Again, the main way we see this happen is firstly by seeking to live lives that model this and then by explaining clearly what the gospel is... and what it isn't!

"Christianity is about being good"

This stems primarily from our sinful human nature, but it's perpetuated by unclear Bible teaching and a social gospel priority of some local churches whose main emphasis is on simply meeting *practical* wants of needy people in our community. We seek to counter this by telling people about the good God who enables us to do good works; pointing back to the giver, not the gifts.

"I just can't trust the Bible"

Many people struggle to accept the authenticity of the Bible, seeing it as an archaic rulebook that bears no relevance to life today. Which makes evangelism tricky when we refer to the Bible as proof for the existence of God! One specific apologetic we have used is to remind people of the great injustice that occurred after the Hillsborough tragedy because the testimony of those who experienced the events was ignored. This has often helped people to understand the importance of eyewitness evidence when dealing with historical documents. More generally – and whether in conversations on the street, Life Groups, Crossroads (our addictions recovery group) or Sunday sermons – what is most powerful is the way that the Bible shows itself to be

God's word as it explains God's world, and as it changes lives. People see their own brokenness, and the brokenness of our community, clearly mirrored in the world of Old and New Testaments, and see change in the lives of their family and friends who have come to know Christ for themselves.

3. As a church, how have you tried to address those issues as you reach out and disciple young believers?

In addition to the above, we're deliberate on Sundays about the way we relate to the brokenness that surrounds us. Our strapline is that we want to be *'a church for people who don't normally go to church'*. We're informal, we start with tea and toast, people come as they are with all their baggage and there's no expectation for them to conform to our way of doing things. This is costly for us and inevitably alienates those who prefer a more conventional way of worshipping. However, we've seen that this approach has helped melt feelings of rejection or unworthiness that people may have experienced in other places.

We seek to treat everyone with dignity by contextualising our evangelistic groups to meet them in their particular struggle or life stage. The addiction support group, mental health befriending group, community drop-in, toddler group and homegroups are all aimed at different people, but the same gospel is explained and applied in all of them.

So far, the people who have come to faith have already been regularly reading the Bible with someone. Once they've made a commitment, we encourage them to continue this discipleship relationship. We also place them into a small group where they can begin serving in church, as we've seen that this is one of the best ways to help new believers flourish.

4. What are the most helpful resources you have found?

BOOKS

- ➡ *Church in Hard Place*s by Mez McConnell & Mike McKinley

- ➡ *Good News for the Poor* by Tim Chester

- ➡ *Instruments in the Redeemer's Hands* by Paul Tripp

WEBSITES

- ➡ 20schemes.com

- ➡ biblicalcounselling.org.uk

- ➡ urbanministries.org.uk

- ➡ citytocityeurope.com

COURSES AND CONFERENCES

- ➡ Certificate in Biblical Counselling from BCUK

- ➡ Biblical Counselling UK Residential Conference

- ➡ Reaching the Unreached Day Conference

MATT WALDOCK is co-pastor of City Church Manchester, an FIEC church he helped plant in 2014. He is married to Jacky and they have a son called Reuben. They live in Ancoats, an area of urban regeneration.

 @mattwaldock

1. How would you describe the community you are seeking to reach?

Manchester is the second fastest growing city in the country and the population explosion has been transformative to the city centre which is being flooded by graduates devouring the plethora of jobs in arts, finance, construction and retail. The diversity of the city is broad with a sizeable Middle Eastern contingent, a growing North African population, the largest UK-based Chinese concentration outside of London and 90,000 university students. Unsurprisingly we have over 36 different nationalities represented at our Sunday Services. However, we're located just off the central square for the city on a street with at least three drug addiction support centres, and our office is a redeemed brothel. One of our four key values is 'accessibility.' Our ten year goal is to see 400-600 people in regular attendance, and our evangelistic strategy is to ensure that a representative cross-section of Manchester's diverse population has access to the gospel through our events.

2. What are the major apologetic challenges or questions you encounter?

Over the last few years there has been a fascinating growth in spiritual curiosity. This is quite new to Manchester which is a city that prides itself on its humanist foundations of industrial and social progress delivered without the necessity of a Christian heritage. As the famous saying in the city goes: "On the sixth day, God created Man*chester*." Now, on the streets of the Northern Quarter no eyebrows would be raised if someone said they believed in God as religion is another life aid alongside yoga or a flat white. However, this spiritual curiosity has developed into an itch to discover something deeper, less vague and more robust to the challenges of life which, given that a significant proportion of the church is on antidepressants, is a prominent issue. Many of the apologetic questions focus upon the tangible impact of Christianity: 'How does being a Christian affect my sense of professional purpose?', or 'How does Christianity answer my chronic loneliness?' And in a culture that is waking up to the consequences of its sexually liberal youth: 'How does Christianity fix my sense of shame?' Apologetics for us is rarely in the terrain of hypotheticals and philosophical abstractions, but rooted in people's real life questions about their intimate pain.

3. As a church, how have you tried to address those issues as you reach out and disciple young believers?

To my surprise it has required us to

cultivate not an armoury of clever answers but, more frighteningly, a necessity to be direct and very personally vulnerable. In our location both young professionals and older folk across racial and ethnic boundaries worship a vague notion of 'authenticity'. No one can agree what it *is* but they know what it *isn't*: it isn't being new or another passing fad; it isn't telling people what they want to hear in order to not offend; and it isn't communicating a message that hasn't cost the speaker something to deliver it. This is an elusive concept on which to build our apologetics strategy, but it seems to be bearing fruit with the church multiplying from 27 in 2014 to around 280 today, with many coming from de-churched backgrounds. Over the last few years we've honed a number of small distinctions that have helped engage the community, but there are a few that have had a significant impact:

1. Our sermons are on average 35-40 minutes in length. Perhaps it helps that it is nearing the same length as average episode length on Netflix, but it enables us to be exegetically rigorous and emotionally colourful in our communication with vivid stories and worked through personal, often confessional examples of the application. A number of people come knowing that they won't agree with what they hear, but they are attracted by the detailed, engaging and sincere presentations that they experience.

2. We regularly use liturgy, creeds and ancient prayers in our services. In our city trends change as often as the weather, and the church operates amongst people and industries desperate to keep up with the latest fresh idea of innovation. Therefore, a sense of depth and rootedness is respected even from non-Christians when we explain the origins of the Athanasian Creed or Heidelberg Catechism. We make a point of intentionally teaching the church, many of them baby Christians, about the history of our faith.

3. Discipleship for us happens communally and centrally rather than being individual and dispersed. From year one our perennial question has been: should we move to small groups in homes? And our answer has always been no, we'll stick with doing everything centrally. In the city centre people tend not to socialise outside of the bars and restaurants; your flat is for sleeping. Besides, the challenge to newcomers crossing the threshold of an apartment block fortress is far harder than a house. So, although we lose the homeliness of distributed small groups, holding 90% of our events in semi-public venues in the heart of the city means that we would have every expectation that a newcomer on Sunday would be with us again on Wednesday or Thursday. Locating our events centrally makes it easier for non-Christians and new or fringe Christians to integrate quickly, both through ease of access and the tangible advert for the Christian community expressed physically through a large gathering of people who want to share their lives together. This is further emphasised by the decision to place a 15 minute refreshments break in the middle of the Service. This both reflects our culture's lack of practice for concentrated sitting through a 90

minute event that doesn't involve a football or Hollywood budget, but also because we aim for every person to have at least one significant conversation before they leave. Meaningful conversations, coupled with a generosity of time for others, in our busy city suggests an authenticity about the church that commends enduring engagement with even the most counter cultural aspects of the gospel.

4. What are the most helpful resources you have found?

With personal suffering and anxiety being front and centre of our apologetic encounters, it has been helpful to intentionally train the church in biblical counselling. We have found that the CCEF materials such as Paul Tripp's *Instruments In The Redeemer's Hands* and Timothy Lane's *How People Change* have been invaluable in equipping us to use biblical counselling as an evangelistic tool. Predominantly this happens with our sermons that intentionally seek to model how the gospel applies to say: depression, eating disorders, social anxiety, anger and workaholism, all of which are commonly experienced

in our community. We brought in a Ministry Trainee who, for two years, was trained in biblical counselling, alongside three other members of staff who have extensively worked through the CCEF material both formally and informally. Each year we hold a day conference for the church called 'Walking Together' that seeks to apply a biblical counselling framework to a handful of pastoral issues that have been prevalent over the last twelve months either within the church or wider community.

We're hungry for new and more accessible resources in this area to more thoroughly strengthen the community and enhance our evangelism. I envisage the need to extend the depth of our provision, because our vision is to be a church-planting church, and one thing that has been apparent over the first few years of City Church is how easily a young plant can get swamped by complex and resource consuming pastoral situations like a dinghy in a storm. In the future, we would love to be involved in providing a biblical counselling hub that would support fledgling churches throughout Manchester.

Find more interviews on this topic on *PrimerHQ.com*, where you can also subscribe to our quarterly email for updates about new issues and resources.